POSTSCRIPT®
LANGUAGE

PROGRAM DESIGN

ADOBE SYSTEMS
INCORPORATED

GLENN C. REID

Addison-Wesley Publishing Company, Inc.

Reading, Massachusetts • Menlo Park, California
New York • Don Mills, Ontario • Wokingham, England
Amsterdam • Bonn • Sydney • Singapore • Tokyo
Madrid • San Juan

Library of Congress Cataloging-in-Publication Data

Postscript language program design / Adobe Systems
Incorporated.

    Includes index.
    ISBN 0-201-14396-8
    1. PostScript (Computer program language)
    I. Adobe Systems.

QA76.73.P67P66 1988   87-36440
005.13'3—dc19   CIP

Printed in the United States of America.
Published simultaneously in Canada.

PostScript is a registered trademark of Adobe Systems
Incorporated.

ISBN 0-201-14396-8
BCDEFGHIJ-HA-898
Second printing: May 1988

CONTENTS

PREFACE

ABOUT THIS BOOK

PostScript® Language Program Design is intended to provide a solid background for developing software in the PostScript language—not just getting a program to work, but thoroughly designing it from top to bottom. The book is organized into fifteen chapters, each of which addresses a specific aspect of program design or problem-solving. The ideas in this book are targeted for sophisticated software development, although they should be useful at any level.

The goal of this book is to teach the fundamentals of designing PostScript programs and to show how the language works, so that your programs will be fast, well-behaved, easy to understand, and portable.

The PostScript language is somewhat unusual in the realm of programming languages in that it is interpreted and stack-based. Learning to program effectively in the PostScript language is not as easy as just learning another procedural high-level language. This book should help you learn how to *think* in the language as well as provide pragmatic advice and examples for accomplishing specific tasks.

The sample programs contained in each chapter are intended to be directly usable. They are examples, but they are not trivial ones. Each program has been carefully designed and debugged and should provide an excellent foundation for an industrial-strength printer driver. Feel free to use the code—that is why it is there.

This volume is a companion volume to two other books by Adobe Systems Incorporated: *PostScript Language Reference Manual* and *PostScript Language Tutorial and Cookbook*, both published by and available from the Addison-Wesley Publishing Company, Inc. We recommend that you have at least the Reference Manual handy when writing programs. If you have not been exposed to the language before, the Tutorial and Cookbook is a good place to start.

PRODUCTION NOTE

Glenn Reid, of Adobe Systems Incorporated, is the principal author of this book. Glenn conceived and executed the text, examples, and illustrations, with feedback from many people at Adobe. John Deubert helped with preliminary outlines of the book and supplied the first draft of Chapter 8. Doug Brotz, Ed Taft, Ann Robinson, Ming Lau, and many others proofread the manuscript, found bugs, and offered valuable advice. Thanks to Carole Alden of Addison-Wesley as editor for providing guidance and encouragement. Special thanks to Pat Marriott, who was a paragon of patience and wisdom throughout the project, and to Linda Gass, who made it all possible.

The book was produced using Frame Maker™ 1.1 from Frame Technologies, Inc., San Jose, California. It was composed and written on a Sun Microsystems™ 3/50 workstation running Sun Unix™. All illustrations were produced in the PostScript language directly with the Adobe Illustrator™ software package on an Apple Macintosh® Plus computer and imported into Frame Maker for final printing. Proofs were printed on a Digital Equipment Corporation ScriptPrinter™ and final camera-ready copy was set on a Linotype L-300 typesetter at Adobe Systems.

PROGRAMMING STYLE AND NOTATION

Programming style is an important part of programming in any language. The PostScript language has a very unstructured syntax and can be somewhat difficult to read, depending on how it is written.

For software development, there are three goals for programming style: the program text should be *readable* (meaning that the structure and execution of the file should be easy to follow), it should be *easily edited*, and it should be *consistent* (especially when more than one programmer is working on the same project). Many reasonable approaches are possible. The style chosen for the listings in this book is designed to be as readable and maintainable as possible without requiring too much white space, which tends to make the listings long and more difficult to read.

PROCEDURE BODIES

Procedure bodies are probably the most common construct in any program written in the PostScript language. Procedure bodies are delimited by braces, also frequently called "curly braces." It is important to be able to determine at a glance where the beginning and end of a procedure body are found. PostScript procedures can be used as arguments for many different operators, including **loop**, **forall**, **kshow**, **image**, **ifelse**, **def**, and others. The notation used for procedures in this book uses a simple PostScript language *comment* to indicate the operator for which the procedure body is an operand:

```
usertime dup 1000 add
{ %loop
        dup usertime lt { pop exit } if
} bind loop
```

Short procedure bodies that fit entirely on one line do not use this comment convention, since their use is more obvious.

INDENTATION

In general, any construct that has a clear beginning and end has its contents indented, including **gsave** and **grestore**, **begin** and **end**, procedure brace delimiters, and so on:

```
/$arithdict 12 dict def
$arithdict begin
    /avg { %def
        add 2 div
    } bind def
    /graph { %def
        gsave
            0 0 moveto
            1 3 avg lineto
            2 setlinecap stroke
        grestore
    } bind def
end % $arithdict
```

The horizontal alignment (indentation) of the beginning of the line containing an open-procedure brace delimiter matches the horizontal alignment of the close brace:

```
currentpoint exch 500 gt { %ifelse
        72 exch 12 sub moveto
}{ %else
        pop
} ifelse
```

The slightly unusual technique of placing brace delimiters on a line by themselves is to make it easier to edit. You can add lines to or subtract lines from procedure bodies without worrying about the delimiters becoming unbalanced.

There are, of course, other styles that work well. This one has been adopted throughout this text so that it is at least consistent, which is the last of the three goals.

THE NAME "POSTSCRIPT"

The name *PostScript*® is a registered trademark of Adobe Systems Incorporated. This book, *PostScript Language Program Design*, is concerned with programs written in the PostScript language. All instances of the name *PostScript* in the text are references to the *PostScript language* as defined by Adobe Systems Incorporated, unless otherwise stated. The name *PostScript* also is used as a product trademark for Adobe Systems' implementation of the PostScript language interpreter.

Any references to a "PostScript printer," a "PostScript file," or a "PostScript driver," refer to printers, files and driver programs (respectively) which are written in or support the PostScript language. The sentences in this book that use "PostScript language" as an adjective phrase are so constructed to reinforce that the name refers to the standard language definition as set forth by Adobe.

PROGRAM DESIGN

chapter 1

THE POSTSCRIPT LANGUAGE: OVERVIEW

*Things should be made as
simple as possible,
but no simpler.*

– Albert Einstein

1.1 INTRODUCTION

PostScript is the name of a computer programming language developed originally by Adobe Systems Incorporated to communicate high-level graphic information to digital laser printers. It is a flexible, compact, and powerful language both for expressing graphic images and for performing general programming tasks.

As is true with many programming languages, the PostScript language has been designed for a specific purpose—to express complex digital graphics in a device-independent manner. Powerful typesetting features are built into the language for sophisticated handling of letterforms as graphics.

The PostScript programming language is an easy one to learn, and graphics programs may be written by hand to produce high quality text and images. However, the language is intended for *machine generation*. That is, PostScript language programs are generally produced by other software rather than by programmers.

This chapter is an overview of some of the more important features of the PostScript language. It is intended to provide a basis for understanding the "why" behind the programming examples given in the rest of the text. The full specification of the PostScript programming language can be found in a companion volume, *PostScript Language Reference Manual* (Addison-Wesley).

It is assumed that the reader of this book is a programmer or has some experience with programming languages. Previous experience with the PostScript language is recommended, but not required. The book is targeted at the specific tasks that need to be performed to implement a driver for any device containing a PostScript interpreter.

The examples in the book are intended to be "cut and paste" routines. They are optimized for efficiency wherever possible, and should be appropriate for direct inclusion in a product-level driver. Rather than making the examples simple and relying on the text to illustrate the point, the *examples* show what you should do, and the text attempts to explain *why*. In theory, at least, it should be possible to paste all the examples in the book together without necessarily understanding how they work and have a very functional program when you are through. In practice, of course, it is best to understand why an example is written the way it is, so that you can adapt the programming style to your own implementation.

Much of the material contained in this book is useful to developers of *drivers* for devices containing PostScript interpreters. A printer driver is typically the part of a software application that produces output specifically intended for a printer. A printer driver for a device with a PostScript interpreter simply produces a PostScript language page description as output, rather than supplying "escape sequences" for a particular printing device. These page descriptions are partly generated by the application software and partially written by hand. This book is dedicated to the process of *design* which must go into producing high-quality PostScript language software.

1.2 THE LANGUAGE MODEL

The three most important aspects of the PostScript programming language are that it is *interpreted*, that it is *stack-based*, and that it uses a unique data structure called a *dictionary*. The dictionary mechanism gives the PostScript language a flexible, extensible base, and the fact that the language is interpreted and uses a stack model means that programs can be of arbitrary length and complexity. Since very little overhead is necessary to execute the programs, they can be interpreted directly from the input stream, which means that no memory restriction is placed on a PostScript language program other than memory allocated by the program itself.

The PostScript language is based heavily on context, or *state*. This context dependency is very powerful—by modifying the coordinate system transformation, any page can be easily scaled, rotated, or translated. The program executes in the context established for it beforehand. By redefining the context of the *dictionary stack* mechanism, built-in PostScript operators can easily be replaced by procedures with additional functionality. Correctly using the context provided by the PostScript imaging model is a challenging aspect of learning the language, since it behaves much differently than most other programming languages in this respect.

The PostScript language is designed to be *interpreted*, not compiled. User programs do not execute directly on the CPU—they are read and interpreted by another program, the *PostScript interpreter*. The PostScript language is a high-level programming language and it can be used to implement algorithms and process data, but a careful understanding is necessary to use it effectively.

The difference in execution speed between a poorly written C program and well written one may be a factor of two or three at best, if the code is improved dramatically. More often, improvements of 10 percent are considered quite good. In general, speed improvements to software written in compiled languages come from improving the algorithms used, not from changing one's programming style.

Simply improving the style of a poorly written PostScript language program can yield substantial execution speed improvements, frequently by a factor of ten or more. The nature of the interpreted language model and the execution semantics require more attention to detail than most compiled languages.

Learning to use the PostScript language well can have an immediate and dramatic effect on the efficiency and reliability of your software.

DICTIONARIES AND DATA STRUCTURES

The PostScript language provides a unique data structure known as a *dictionary*. A dictionary is a structure in which are stored *key–value* pairs, where the key and the value can be any valid PostScript language objects. Presenting a key (usually a *name object*) to the PostScript interpreter will cause it to perform a name lookup, and execute the resulting object found in the dictionary. This mechanism provides an extremely flexible foundation for the language. New procedures can easily be created, and existing operator names can be redefined.

The PostScript language also provides several other standard data structures: strings, arrays (of any PostScript objects, including other arrays), integers, reals, names (analogous to identifiers in other languages), and files (with standard file operations defined). All of these data types are maintained as PostScript objects, which are manipulated on the operand stack. A dictionary can contain any of these data types as a value. The notion of a *variable* usually means a dictionary entry in the PostScript language.

A PostScript dictionary is the *only* way to store PostScript objects for later recall (other than leaving a reference to them on the operand stack). The standard operator for making a dictionary entry is the **def** operator, which makes a *definition* in the current dictionary. This mechanism is used for conventional purposes such as defining and using variables or procedures, but it can also be used for more complex data structures.

STACKS

The PostScript language is based on stacks. A *stack* is a fixed data structure in which objects are placed temporarily, one on top of another. By nature, stacks are "last in, first out" data structures. If you put three items on a stack, the third one is on the top, (and is the first item available).

Operators in the PostScript language are *preceded* by their operands. The operands are placed on the operand stack as they are encountered by the interpreter, and when the operator itself is encountered and executed, its arguments are found on the stack. This is often referred to as *post-fix* notation.

There are several stacks used by the PostScript interpreter—an *operand* stack, an *execution* stack, a *dictionary* stack, and a *graphics state* stack. The operand stack is in constant use, while the others are more specialized. The operand stack is frequently referred to simply as "the stack."

Programming in the PostScript language is primarily an exercise in stack manipulation. The most common PostScript errors result from incorrect manipulation of the stack, and many optimization strategies consist of using the stack as efficiently as possible. Further discussion of stack mechanics is provided in Chapter 2. It is worthwhile to become quite familiar with the mechanics of stack operations in the PostScript language.

BUILT-IN POSTSCRIPT LANGUAGE OPERATORS

The standard PostScript interpreter has more than 250 built-in operators. It is an extremely rich language. The nature of the PostScript language's execution model makes it very easy to add new procedures that behave like operators, since the interface between them is just the operand stack.

It is difficult to learn how to use 262 operators at first. It is even harder to remember all of them. However, using the appropriate operator for the task at hand can be very important in terms of performance and program design As a rule of thumb, keep the following in mind:

> *If you are having difficulty with some aspect of your program, it is likely that the problem has been encountered before. There may be a specific PostScript language operator that directly addresses the problem. It is a good idea to briefly review a list of operators grouped by function when you encounter problems. (See chapter 6 of the* PostScript Language Reference Manual.*)*

1.3   THE IMAGING MODEL

The *imaging model* of the PostScript language includes standard operations for typesetting and rendering graphics. The model is device- and resolution-independent, and provides an abstraction for raster imaging that frees application software from having to make device-specific rendering decisions.

An important aspect of using the PostScript language correctly is to make proper use of the imaging model. The purpose of the PostScript language is to provide a uniform way to represent visual elements on any raster device. An application program typically needs to communicate visually with the user in terms of representing text, graphics, and aspects of the user interface. Whatever internal representation or data structure is used, some imaging model is necessary when presenting the information visually.

When printing on a device with a PostScript interpreter, some translation is usually necessary between the applications internal representation for graphics and the PostScript language's imaging model, unless the screen display is also driven by a PostScript interpreter.

The PostScript language provides both an execution model and an imaging model to applications programs. An important consideration is to adapt naturally to the imaging model when producing output for the PostScript interpreter, rather than using the programming power of the language to emulate another graphic imaging model.

COORDINATE SYSTEMS

The *user coordinate system* in the PostScript imaging model provides a consistent and predictable environment for constructing graphics. This coordinate system, referred to as *user space*, is the same for all printers with PostScript interpreters—it is only the mapping from user space to *device space* that is different from one raster device to another, depending on the resolution and orientation of the device.

To produce truly device-independent programs with the PostScript language, it is important to think only in terms of the user space abstraction, and never about any particular output device. Similarly, page layout and sizes should be expressed only in terms of where they fall in user space. The coordinate system transformation from user space into device space can be modified easily to scale an entire page when it is actually rendered, and it is good not to make any specific assumptions at page composition time about the size of the final page.

PATHS AND PAINT

Graphics in the PostScript language are rendered by constructing algorithmic *paths* consisting of lines, arcs of circles, or Beziér curves. These paths are then *painted* with a current color or grayscale (the default color is black). Paths may also be used for clipping or masking graphics, and they may be either stroked with a line, filled as regions, or both.

Paint is applied to the current page as opaque color, completely painting over anything that may be beneath it on the current page. There is a more detailed discussion of this in Chapter 3.

FONTS

The PostScript language has a completely integrated model for quality typesetting. PostScript fonts are executable programs that draw the character shapes using the same path construction and painting mechanism as all other graphics. The text can be thought of as integrated graphics, and can be transformed in any way that graphics can be. There is extensive support in the PostScript language (beyond the standard graphics commands) for manipulating font programs and for setting text characters.

Fonts may be created from existing graphic shapes. Once a program or procedure has been devised that renders a particular shape, that code can be packaged into a font dictionary and placed on the page through the text-handling mechanisms.

It is the representation of typefaces as graphic descriptions that realizes the full integration of text and graphics on a single page. It is not that the text alone may be scaled and rotated that is significant—it is that the entire page is completely integrated and may be treated as a single graphic entity, and the page itself may be printed half-size or rotated to any angle.

1.4 ELECTRONIC PUBLISHING AND PRINTING

Electronic publishing is the business of composing and printing documents, from books to magazines and even newsletters.

Computers are now used extensively to simplify the editing, composition, and typesetting of books and documents.

The PostScript language is a *system solution* to the perplexing problem of composing, proofing, and printing documents. It is intended chiefly for high quality typesetting, graphic design, and book production. However it is also used for more standard computer printing, including everything from program listings to business correspondence using typewriter-like typefaces.

There are many, many different levels at which a computer environment might support PostScript technology. A PostScript printer may be used to get "hard copy" of something on the computer screen, it may be used to print text in much the same way that a line printer does, or the PostScript language typesetting and graphic models may be used fully in the preparation of camera-ready output for major book production.

There is a great difference between printed output intended as a final product and simply a "hard copy" of some information that already exists in some other form.

When designing software, it is useful to consider what the *final product* will be. If the program is a word processor, for instance, is the final product considered to be the words themselves, their arrangement, the typeface that they are set in, or the book in which they will eventually appear? To enter even slightly into the level of *presentation* means a heavy commitment to the final form. For example, if the arrangement of words is part of the product, then it becomes a *visual* product, and most likely a *printed* visual product.

When designing software for printing and publishing, the final-form technology must be considered. The graphic imaging model used by the printing technology, the available typefaces, the units of measure, and the available paper sizes are all part of the final product.

A common problem in bridging from traditional computer printing into the realm of electronic publishing is to muddy the waters between *composing* the document and *printing* it. For example, when printing on PostScript devices, one must compose text using the character widths of the fonts that will ultimately be used on the printer. This requires some advance knowledge of the printing technology. But it is the *abstraction* that is used, and not a particular output device. The resolution and printing characteristics of the device should not be propagated into the document design—only the *ideals* of the layout.

1.5 PROGRAM DESIGN GUIDELINES

There are a few items that may be kept in mind while implementing a driver for a PostScript device. As with most software development, the most difficult part of writing programs in the PostScript language is the *design* of the program. If the design is good, implementing it is easy. If the design is poor, it may not even be possible to correctly implement it. Below are some helpful items to keep in mind when writing your software. All of them are explained more fully within the text of this book; this is only an attempt to prime the pump before you start reading:

- Use the operand stack efficiently. Pay particular attention to the order of the elements on the stack and how they are used.

- Avoid unnecessary redundancy. When a program is produced, check for many repetitive steps that perhaps could be condensed. Keep identifiers short if they are to be transmitted many times.

- Use the PostScript imaging model effectively. When printing, a document must be translated into the language of the printer. This includes a philosophical adjustment to the nature of the PostScript imaging model.

- It is better to translate into the PostScript imaging model than to maintain another set of graphics primitives using the PostScript language for emulation.

chapter 2

THE EXECUTION MODEL

It is more of a job to interpret the
interpretations than to interpret the things,
and there are more books about books
than about any other subject....

– *Michel Eyquem de Montaigne*

2.1 INTRODUCTION

The manner in which the PostScript interpreter executes a program has a profound effect on the efficiency and design of software. This chapter takes a close look at the execution semantics and details of the PostScript interpreter, with the idea that a full understanding of how a program is being executed will provide a solid foundation for good programming skills. Probably the most important concept to glean from this chapter is the notion of PostScript language *objects* and how they are stored and manipulated. Understanding the mechanics of the scanner and interpreter will also help shed light on issues of efficiency.

2.2 THE PRINTING JOB MODEL

PostScript interpreters are most frequently used in *batch mode*. That is, a document is prepared by applications software and is then submitted to a PostScript printer for interpretation. A document may consist of any number of pages and any amount of text and graphical information, since interpretation is carried out directly as the file is received by the interpreter.

For example, it is typical to start with a page composition program that permits users to construct pages, graphics, and text interactively. The PostScript language may be used for display purposes during the document composition, but it is likely to be an interactive session. When the document is to be printed, the application invokes a particular section of code usually known as a *printer driver* to produce the output for the printing device. This page description must then be transmitted to the printer as a batch job, usually by an intermediate communications filter. The print job is then scanned and interpreted by the PostScript interpreter for that printer, and the resulting pages are printed.

This model of execution is mostly invisible when one creates and executes PostScript language programs. It is presented here as a framework of reference, since it is the outermost level of interpretation in a device with a PostScript interpreter.

A PostScript interpreter (in batch mode) executes a single *job* from the time it receives the initial byte over a communications channel through the next *end-of-file* (EOF) indication. All legal PostScript language sequences are interpreted and executed by the interpreter until the EOF is reached. At the end of each job, the interpreter resets the state which existed at the beginning of the job. This is actually accomplished by the **save** and **restore** operators. The interpreter then returns to an idle state until the next job is received. This behavior is discussed in more detail in Section 2.9, "THE SERVER LOOP." This job execution model has two important consequences:

- The PostScript interpreter is completely restored to its original state after each job finishes execution.

- Each print job must be a contiguous stream of bytes. Anything that is to be part of a particular document must be present in the print file.

The main advantage of this mechanism is that it guarantees certain initial state conditions to all print jobs, regardless of whether the job is the first or the forty-first one interpreted since the machine was powered on. A print job should always assume that the initial state of the PostScript interpreter is the default state, which is defined in Section 6.3, "MODULARITY AND PAGE STRUCTURE." This initial state is guaranteed by the job server loop.

For reasons that will become apparent, it is important to trust the initial state of the interpreter. A common practice is to initialize the interpreter at the beginning of each job, in an attempt to guarantee some execution state for the job. In most instances, this accomplishes nothing. (The state has already been initialized by the server loop). In instances where the state is *not* the default state, there is likely to be a good reason for it. For example, the transformation matrix may have been modified to print the page as a small illustration rather than as a full-size page. Initializing the matrix will reverse this effect. For a more involved discussion of this principle, see Section 6.3 and most of Chapter 11.

2.3 THE OPERAND STACK

The *operand stack* is, in a sense, the global communications area for execution and parameter passing in the PostScript language. All data objects that are to be operated on by any procedure or operator must be present on the operand stack. Objects are placed on the operand stack by the PostScript interpreter. As a rule of thumb, *any object that is not directly executable* is placed on the operand stack. There are a few special exceptions to this, which are detailed throughout this chapter.

OBJECTS IN THE POSTSCRIPT LANGUAGE

An *object* is actually a unified representation used for all entities in the PostScript language. Each object is a fixed-size package (in many implementations it is 8 bytes, for example). Since these objects are all the same size, they are easily manipulated on the operand stack, placed into dictionaries, and passed through the internal mechanisms of the PostScript interpreter. There are two distinct kinds of objects, simple and composite.

A *simple object* is one whose value can be stored within the 8-byte packet that represents the object. These include the data types *integer, mark, real, boolean, name,* and *null.* Each of these data types can be represented in a self-contained object.

A *composite object* is one whose value is stored elsewhere in memory. The object itself contains a pointer to the value, which in turn can consist of other objects. Only the data types *string, dictionary,* and *array* are composite objects. A procedure body is actually just an executable array, so procedure bodies also qualify as composite objects.

To understand the distinction between a simple and a composite object, consider what happens when the **dup** operator is executed. The **dup** operator makes a copy of (duplicates) the top entry on the operand stack. Since the operand stack contains only objects, the result of executing **dup** is to duplicate the object itself.

If the topmost object on the operand stack is a simple object, **dup** produces a new object with a copy of the original value, since the object is completely self-contained. With a composite object, however, the new object produced by **dup** contains a pointer to the same value as the original. The value of the object is stored elsewhere in memory, and is *not* duplicated. This means that any changes made to the value of the duplicated copy are also made to the original. You can obtain a new, distinct copy by allocating a new composite object (with the **dict**, **string**, or **array** operators, for example) and using the **copy** operator to copy the original object's value to the new one.

Another way to think of it is that the *value* stored with an object either fits into the object (simple) or it doesn't. If it doesn't, then a pointer to the value is stored instead (composite). See Figure 2.1.

figure 2.1

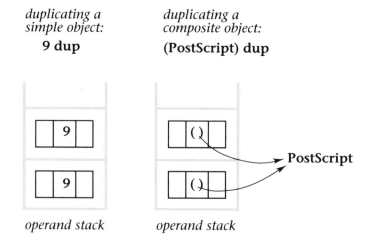

duplicating a simple object:

9 dup

duplicating a composite object:

(PostScript) dup

operand stack　　　*operand stack*

Each object has several *attributes* associated with it. These include a *literal* or *executable* flag, an *access* attribute, which controls read-write-execute permissions for the object, and a *length* attribute (used only with composite objects). There is also a *type* associated with every object as one of its attributes. Some of these attributes are easily changed with the following operators:

Attributes	Operators
literal/executable	**cvlit, cvx**
access	**readonly**
	executeonly
	noaccess
type	**cvi, cvr, cvrs**
	cvs, cvn

For the most part, there is no need to convert objects from one type to another or to modify their attributes. However, it is good to remember that PostScript language objects are *typed* and maintained internally with this representation.

THE STACK AS A DATA STRUCTURE

The operand stack is often overlooked as a data structure for program development. In fact, it is the fastest, most direct, cheapest, and easiest-to-use data structure available in the PostScript language.

The techniques for using the stack effectively are many. Almost without exception, the sample programs in this book use the operand stack directly instead of defining local storage. Since all objects are initially constructed on the operand stack when they are read from the input stream, the most natural approach is to use them directly from the stack. Resist the temptation to define variables for procedure operands, unless those values are needed more than once or twice. This is related to the fundamental design issues of how and when to pass values on the stack, when to use the graphics state stack, and when to use "global variables." For further discussion on program organization, please see Chapter 5.

Objects that are placed on the operand stack should be in a natural order appropriate for their intended use. To understand this, consider the two (equivalent) PostScript language fragments given in *listing 2-1*; each takes the same values on the operand stack, but each in a different order. Compare the procedures and how they use the data.

listing 2-1 ───────────────────────────────

```
%!PS-Adobe-2.0
%%Title: stack example
/procGOOD { %def
    findfont exch scalefont setfont
} bind def
/procOK { %def
    exch findfont exch scalefont setfont
} bind def
/procBAD { %def
    /ptsize exch def
    /fontname exch def
    fontname findfont ptsize scalefont
    setfont
} bind def
%%EndProlog
12 /StoneSerif  procGOOD
/StoneSerif 12  procOK
/StoneSerif 12  procBAD
%%Trailer
```

───

The procedure calls themselves look much the same. The data passed is identical in each case. The difference between the **procGOOD** and **procOK** procedures is only a single **exch** instruction. However, if the data is supplied in the natural order, the **exch** is unnecessary. The only difference between **procGOOD** and **procBAD** is that the operand stack is used naturally in the good example, whereas the operands are defined into a dictionary (and subsequently retrieved from the dictionary and put back on the operand stack) in the bad example.

2.4 THE DICTIONARY STACK

The *dictionary stack* is a very special feature of the PostScript language. It is the *context* in which name lookup and definitions occur. It can be manipulated directly, but it is best to think of it as an environment, not a data structure.

The dictionary stack contains objects, just as the operand stack does. However, the only type of object which can be placed on the dictionary stack is, naturally, a dictionary object.

DICTIONARY OBJECTS

A dictionary is a composite object, much like an array. It is represented by a *dictionary object*, and it is always referenced through that object. The object can be placed onto one of the stacks, or it can be stored in a dictionary, just like any other object. However, certain special operations can be performed *only* with dictionaries. In particular, entries in a dictionary are *ordered pairs*. Each entry has a *key* and a *value* (actually an object, not to be confused with the *value* of the object itself). Either of these objects can itself be a composite object, including a dictionary.

Dictionaries are the foundation of the storage and retrieval mechanism in the PostScript language. Data can actually exist in only one of two places:

- On the operand stack (or as a component of a composite object on the operand stack)

- In a dictionary (or in a component of a dictionary, such as an array).

The reason is that unless an object is on one of the stacks, the only way to call it up is by name. If you don't store something explicitly into a dictionary (with **def**, for instance) and the object is removed from the operand stack, it *cannot be recovered*. That alone is not quite reason enough to place something in a dictionary, but it is something to be aware of.

Dictionary objects can be created only by the **dict** operator. The **dict** operator requires an integer value as its argument, and it creates an empty dictionary object with that number of elements allocated for later use. The dictionary object is returned on the operand stack. For example, the dictionary created by the sequence **3 dict** is just a composite object. It is not the current dictionary, nor does it have a name. It is just an empty data structure on the operand stack, which (in this instance) can contain up to three entries.

USING THE DICTIONARY STACK

The dictionary stack starts out with two entries. These are known as **systemdict** and **userdict**. These dictionaries cannot be removed from the dictionary stack. The **systemdict** dictionary contains predefined names for all the standard PostScript language operators. The other dictionary, **userdict**, is a writable dictionary that typically has about 200 elements available. **userdict** is on the top of the dictionary stack when each job begins, and **systemdict** is right below it. The dictionaries on the dictionary stack are the context in which name lookup takes place. You can use this mechanism to redefine built-in PostScript language operators or to define new procedures, as appropriate. The name-lookup mechanism is described in Section 2.5.

Other dictionary objects can be placed onto the dictionary stack with the **begin** operator. It is called **begin** because it affects the context in which dictionary operations take place. Its effect is to place a dictionary object on top of the dictionary stack, making it the current dictionary. The current dictionary is simply the one on top of the dictionary stack.

The *current dictionary* is where definitions are placed when the **def** operator is executed. It is also the first place the interpreter looks when a name lookup takes place. Let's look at a PostScript language sequence that creates and uses a dictionary:

```
3 dict begin
 /proc1 { pop } def
 /two 2 def
 /three (trois) def
currentdict
end
```

This example creates a dictionary with three available slots, places it on the dictionary stack (with **begin**, making it the current dictionary), and then makes three definitions (with **def**). The definitions are placed into the newly created dictionary only because it was made the current dictionary, not because it was recently created. The call to **currentdict** makes a copy of the dictionary object (the one currently on top of the dictionary stack) and places the copy on the operand stack. Notice that the dictionary object that was initially created was also on the operand stack until **begin** moved it to the dictionary stack. The **end** operator simply pops one element off the dictionary stack (and discards it). If **currentdict** had not been executed before **end**, the dictionary (along with its three entries) *would have been lost*. This is because the object created by the **3 dict** statement was never stored into a dictionary—it was simply used by the **begin** operator. Here is an equivalent (though substantively different) PostScript language fragment:

> **3 dict**
> **dup /proc1 { pop } put**
> **dup /two 2 put**
> **dup /three (trois) put**

This examples uses **put** instead of **def**. It never places the dictionary onto the dictionary stack, and it makes each entry explicitly by presenting the dictionary object to the **put** operator each time. (The **dup** is used to avoid losing the object when **put** is performed.) However, the resulting dictionary on the operand stack is identical to the one created in the previous example.

The dictionary stack is an environment. It is most important as a context for name lookup, which is discussed in depth in the next section. The previous discussion, although cumbersome, is meant to illustrate two concepts:

- Dictionaries are represented as *objects*, which can either be left on one of the stacks or given a name and defined as an entry in another dictionary.

- Dictionary objects do not necessarily have names and are much like arrays in their use. They are special mostly in the context of name lookup.

2.5 OPERATORS AND NAME LOOKUP

All built-in PostScript language operators are stored in dictionaries as executable objects of type **operatortype**. The keys under which these operators are stored are the names by which we think of them: **moveto**, **showpage**, or **add**, for example. The names themselves are not special in any way. They are used simply as *keys* for dictionary entries. (For the most part, they are keys in **systemdict**.) The actual execution is carried out after these names have been looked up and an executable object has been found in **systemdict**. This mechanism is known as *automatic name lookup*.

Name lookup is invoked whenever the PostScript interpreter encounters an *executable name object*. The difference between a *literal name* and an executable name in the PostScript language is the presence (or absence) of a leading slash character:

/**moveto**   % literal name

moveto   % executable name

When the PostScript interpreter encounters an executable name, it looks up the name in the current dictionary context and interprets whatever it finds as a result of that name lookup.

figure 2.2

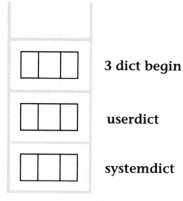

3 dict begin

userdict

systemdict

dictionary stack

Name lookup is done from the top down, in the context of the current dictionary stack. When a name is encountered (whether it is in the original input file or found in a procedure body executed later) it is looked up in all dictionaries that are currently on the dictionary stack. (See figure 2.2.)

If the interpreter finds an executable object (like a procedure body) or a built-in PostScript language operator, it executes it directly, rather than placing it on the operand stack. This is how both operators and procedures are executed: They are just looked up in a dictionary as names, and the object found in the dictionary is interpreted further.

THE **BIND** OPERATOR

The **bind** operator is used to perform *early name binding* on procedure bodies. What this means, effectively, is that it is possible to look up all the names in a procedure ahead of time and, if a real operator is found (as opposed to an array, a procedure, or any other type of object), to replace the executable name with the operator itself. This is a very important concept in making PostScript programs more efficient. The resulting procedure body (after **bind** is applied) may actually have its contents modified. Here is a sample use:

```
%!PS-Adobe-2.0
/F { %def
        findfont exch scalefont setfont
} bind def
%%EndProlog
12 /StoneInformal F
```

When **bind** is executed, there are two things on the operand stack: a literal name, /**F**, and a procedure body, { **findfont exch scalefont setfont** }. The **bind** operator returns an array object on the stack when it is finished. In this case, however, since none of the operators in the procedure have previously been redefined, **bind** finds real operators (objects of type /**operatortype**) for every name lookup except **findfont**, which is actually a procedure. The result looks something like this:

{ **findfont --exch-- --scalefont-- --setfont--** }

The --**setfont**-- notation with the hyphens is a convention used by the == operator to indicate an object of type /**operatortype** (as distinguished from an executable name). It means that the name objects have been removed and replaced by operator objects. The array as it is stored in memory actually looks like *figure 2.3*:

figure 2.3

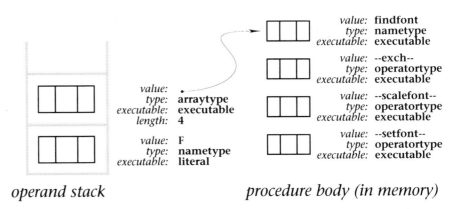

operand stack   procedure body (in memory)

The procedure body is actually an array object with its executable flag set, and the contents of the array are, in turn, other objects. After **bind** is applied, the original name objects are replaced by their respective operator objects, as you can see in the figure.

It is useful to execute **bind** on any procedure body that will be used many times. The result of binding a procedure body is that the name-lookup operations can be distilled out, requiring less time to execute the procedure. The semantics of **bind** dictate that if an operator has been redefined prior to being used in a procedure, then **bind** leaves the name in the procedure body and will *not* replace it with the operator object.

```
/showpage { } def
/ENDPAGE { %def
    gsave
        showpage    % name is not replaced
    grestore
} bind def
```

```
/ENDPAGE { %def
        gsave
            showpage    % name is replaced by operator
        grestore
} bind def
/showpage { } def   % has no effect in ENDPAGE proc
```

Because **bind** replaces only those items that are found to be of type **operatortype**, it will not replace an object that is of type **arraytype** (which is the case when an operator name is redefined with a user procedure). This means simply that it is all right to bind procedures even if some of their elements might be redefined, as long as the definitions are done *before* the procedures are called.

2.6   THE INTERPRETER AND THE SCANNER

The PostScript interpreter deals only with *objects*. A separate entity exists between the interpreter and the standard input stream known as the *scanner*. The scanner actually converts incoming bytes into objects and hands them to the interpreter. It is invoked directly by the interpreter whenever more information is needed from the input stream. (Note that the scanner does not *pre-scan* any of the incoming bytes, since they could be used as data and not read by the interpreter.)

The scanner actually tokenizes the input stream into PostScript objects. This includes conversion of names into name objects and strings into string objects. It is the scanner that makes the distinction between a literal and an executable name by recognizing the leading slash character ("/"). Thus the distinction between /**findfont** and **findfont** is made by the scanner, which sets the literal or executable flag on the resulting name object.

The scanner recognizes strings (with either the (*string*) or <*string*> notation) and converts them into string objects. The scanner also recognizes the backslash notation in string objects (including \\, \(, \), and *octal* notation). For example, if it encounters a sequence like the following:

(\101B\103D \\\(ABCD\) (balanced))

the scanner will recognize and replace the backslash notation with the appropriate characters and it will produce a string object as follows. The parentheses are omitted because they are not part of the string, but indications to the scanner of where the string starts and end (although this string contains some parentheses as data, as you can see):

ABCD \(ABCD) (balanced)

The scanner also is responsible for issuing the PostScript language **syntaxerror**, which can only result from mismatched (unbalanced) string delimiters and unexpected ends-of-file. There are no other syntax errors possible in the PostScript language!

The PostScript interpreter invokes the scanner each time it needs a token from the object currently being executed. The scanner reads from a file or string with exactly the same semantics as the **token** operator (see the *PostScript Language Reference Manual*), returning exactly one object to the interpreter.

RECOGNITION OF OBJECTS

It is the scanner's responsibility to recognize objects. There are only four kinds of objects that it knows how to recognize:

- *Literal strings*: any string object delimited by either < > or ( ). The scanner watches for \ notation and attempts to find the closing delimiter. Mismatched delimiters result in **syntaxerror**.

- *Numbers*: the scanner tries first to make a number out of a token. This includes reals, integers, and radix notation.

- *Names*: anything that cannot be interpreted as one of the above is returned as a name object. The literal/executable flag is set depending on the presence of a leading slash (/).

- *Procedure bodies*: Procedure bodies delimited by curly braces '{ }' are recognized by the scanner and returned to the interpreter as executable array objects.

chapter 2 THE EXECUTION MODEL

There are a few special cases. For instance, the leading slash (indicating a literal name) overrides the scanner's ability to recognize a token as a number:

> **/1000 type ==**
> *nametype*

It is worth noting that any type of object can be used as a key in a dictionary. Names are used most often, but they are not required. The following is a perfectly legal, although somewhat confusing, PostScript language sequence (shown as though typed in interactive mode):

> **PS> 13 (thirteen) def**
> **PS> 13 load ==**
> **(thirteen)**
> **PS>**

It is necessary to use **load** in this example because the token **13** is recognized first as an integer, not as a name. Therefore, automatic name lookup is not invoked. The **load** operator explicitly invokes key lookup for any object, in the context of the current dictionary stack.

Note:

> *When a name is encountered in a program, the scanner returns a name object. Name objects require a fixed amount of overhead, regardless of the number of bytes in the name. However, time required to recognize a name is proportional to its length. With this in mind, it is always best to use short procedure names if the procedure will be invoked many times (as in the script, but not in the prologue—see Section 6.2).*

2.7 PROCEDURES

A PostScript language *procedure* is simply an executable array of PostScript objects. Normally, procedures are given a name and stored in a dictionary, so that they may be called up by presenting the appropriate executable name to the PostScript interpreter. However, procedures can exist without having names at all (as can any object until it is stored into a dictionary).

A procedure that exists (perhaps on the operand stack) but is not referenced by name is typically referred to as a *procedure body*. Procedure bodies are usually stored in a dictionary under a particular name and used in the same manner as the built-in operators, although they are also required (or permitted) as arguments to several operators, including **image, imagemask, setscreen, settransfer, if, ifelse, loop,** and **forall**.

The PostScript language's mechanism for building and defining a procedure is worth examining more closely:

> /**F** { %def
>   **findfont exch scalefont setfont**
> } **bind def**

This is a typical procedure definition. It builds a procedure body (in this case consisting mostly of operators), executes **bind** to distill out the name lookup, and then defines the procedure in the current dictionary under the name **F**.

Let's look at this sequence as the PostScript interpreter would, token by token:

> /**F**

The scanner digests this as a literal name object and hands it to the interpreter. The PostScript interpreter places all literal objects directly on the operand stack and moves on.

> {

This is a special PostScript language delimiter (informally known as a "curly brace," or "open-curly"). It marks the beginning of a procedure body. The scanner enters *deferred execution* mode when this character is encountered. All objects through the closing '}' token are scanned but not executed, regardless of their type. When the closing delimiter is found, an executable array is created containing all the collected objects between the '{ }' delimiters.

In most implementations, the scanner uses the operand stack to construct procedure bodies, placing a **mark** on the stack and then placing each object on the operand stack until the closing brace is found, at which point the array is constructed from the objects on the stack. This places a practical limitation on the number of objects (which may be composite objects) which can be put into a procedure. In most implementations, this number is 499, which is the depth of the operand stack less 1 for the **mark** (*listing 2-3* contains a method for building much larger procedure bodies when necessary). Here is the state of the stack just before the '}' character is encountered, which causes the objects on the stack (down through the **mark**) to be collapsed into a single array object.

setfont

scalefont

exch

findfont

--mark--

/F

These are all objects of type **/nametype**, with the exception of the mark, which is of **/marktype**. The scanner performs no name lookups during the scanning of a procedure body.

When the scanner recognizes the '}' delimiter it performs several functions. First, it decrements the level counter that keeps track of the nesting of curly braces, and if the level is back to 0, the interpreter reverts back to immediate execution mode (which is the normal state of the PostScript interpreter). Next, the scanner performs the equivalent of **counttomark array astore**: It allocates an array of the appropriate length, fills it with the objects on the stack down through the **mark**, removes the **mark**, and leaves a freshly created array object on the stack.

The final step is to make the new array an executable array. (It does this by performing the equivalent of **cvx**.) Here is the state of the operand stack right after the '}' character is processed:

--executable array--

/F

The name /F is still on the bottom of the operand stack, where it was at the beginning of this example. The entire procedure body is now stored in memory as a sequence of objects represented as an executable array object on the operand stack. Note that there is still no procedure named F. There are merely two objects on the operand stack. They could be eliminated very easily by executing the **clear** or **pop** operators, for example. It is not until the **def** operator is finally executed that this array object is safely stored in the current dictionary under the name F. The remaining part of the last line of the program is

bind def

These are two more executable names. Each of these is looked up and executed (since the interpreter is now in immediate execution mode). The effect of executing **bind** is to perform *early name binding* on any elements of the array object that may be executable operator names. (See Section 2.5, "OPERATORS AND NAME LOOKUP," for a discussion of **bind**.) The **bind** operator expects to find an executable array on the operand stack, and it leaves one there (possibly containing different objects) when it is through.

The effect of executing **def**, of course, is to take the top two elements from the operand stack and make a *key-value* pair association in the current dictionary. The F procedure is now defined. It can be used like any of the built-in operators in the PostScript language, as long as the dictionary in which it is stored is available on the dictionary stack.

listing 2-2 ————————————————————————

```
%!PS-Adobe-2.0
/F { %def
        findfont exch scalefont setfont
} bind def
%%EndProlog
```

```
24 /Helvetica F
288 72 moveto
(Green Book) show
showpage
```

Listing 2-2 would result in something like this being printed on the page:

Green Book

VERY LARGE PROCEDURE BODIES

Occasionally one needs to define a very large procedure body, perhaps as a character description in a font or as part of a logotype. The operand stack depth limit is typically about 500 elements, which limits the total size of a procedure created while in deferred execution mode, since all the elements in the procedure are first placed on the operand stack.

There are a few ways to cope with this problem. The easiest way, if the host application can keep track of how many elements are being generated, is to break out pieces of the procedure and make them separate procedures, invoked by name within the large procedure body:

```
/small1 { one two three four } def
/small2 { five six seven eight } def
/small3 { nine ten eleven twelve } def
/large {
      small1 small2 small3
} def
```

If the procedure is being generated automatically, rather than by hand, this may not be a feasible approach. For one thing, the number of new (unique) names required cannot be predicted easily. In *listing 2*-3 is a method for collapsing a large procedure into many small component pieces.

listing 2-3

```
%!PS-Adobe-2.0
%%Title: collapseproc.ps
%%EndComments
/EXEC { /exec load } bind def
/mainproc [  %def
     { gsave 400 36 moveto } EXEC
     { /Times-Italic findfont 24 } EXEC
     { scalefont setfont (from Listing 2-3) } EXEC
     { show grestore } EXEC
] cvx bind def
%%EndProlog
mainproc
showpage
%%Trailer
```

Notice the use of **exec** in this example. It is necessary since the component procedure bodies will not be immediately executed when encountered directly (they are simply placed on the operand stack). Also, the relationship between building square bracket arrays and curly-brace procedure bodies is interesting (and crucial to this example). Since the outermost brackets are actually *square brackets*, all the intervening PostScript code is executed, not deferred. For this reason, in order to place the **exec** operator in the procedure body, its value must be obtained with **load** (see the **EXEC** procedure in the example). Here is what the /**mainproc** in *listing 2-3* looks like after it is built (a little interactive dialog is shown to show the length of the array, too):

```
PS> /mainproc load dup ==
{ { gsave 400 36 moveto } --exec-- { /Times-Italic
  findfont 24 } --exec-- { scalefont setfont
  (from Listing 2-3) } --exec-- { show grestore }
  --exec-- }
PS> length ==
8
PS>
```

Each procedure body within the square brackets is built individually, and when the '}' token is encountered, each one is collapsed into a single (executable) array object on the operand stack. This way the operand stack does not overflow, since it is effectively segmented into smaller pieces. An *array of arrays* is built, and each sub-array is explicitly executed by **exec**. The outermost array is simply made executable and can be used like any other procedure.

listing 2-4 ─────────────────────────────────────

```
%!PS-Adobe-2.0
%%Title: addproc.ps
%%EndComments
/F { findfont exch scalefont setfont } bind def
/S { moveto show } bind def
/addprocs {  %def
      dup length 2 add array cvx
      dup 3 -1 roll 2 exch putinterval
      dup 0 4 -1 roll put
      dup 1 /exec load put
} bind def
%%EndProlog
gsave
      currenttransfer { 1 exch sub } addprocs
      settransfer
      36 /Helvetica-Oblique F
      1 setgray  % normally white...
      (Black) 36 670 S    % but the inverse transfer
      (Words) 36 634 S  % function yields black
grestore
showpage
%%Trailer
```

───

Another application of this technique is a space-efficient way to concatenate two procedure bodies, as can be seen in *listing 2-4*. It defines a procedure called **addprocs** which concatenates two existing procedure bodies. It creates one new procedure body that is the length of the second procedure plus two. The array object representing the first procedure is inserted into the *0th* position in the new array, the **exec** operator is placed in the second slot, and the second procedure is copied into the rest of the new procedure body, resulting in a new procedure like this:

{ one two three } { four five six } addprocs

=> { { **one two three** } **exec four five six** }

This preserves at least the first of the procedures without having to copy it (it is simply executed with **exec**).

2.8   THE EXECUTION STACK

The PostScript interpreter always looks at the top of the *execution stack* when it has finished executing any single operator. The execution stack contains the object currently being executed, whether it is a procedure body, the standard input file, some other file object, or a string. During the normal execution of a print job, there is a file object on the execution stack that represents the standard input file, and as the program is executed, other procedure bodies may also be placed on top of the execution stack temporarily until they have been completely executed.

Objects can explicitly be placed on the execution stack with the **exec**, **run**, or **stopped**, **for**, **ifelse**, and **forall** operators. Each of these causes an object to be executed directly. If the object is a file or string, it is tokenized first by the scanner. If the object is an executable array (a procedure body), each object in the array is executed consecutively. If the object is a file, it is scanned and interpreted and the file object is popped from the execution stack when the end-of-file indication is reached.

There is an infinite loop on the bottom of the execution stack, known as the *server loop*. (See the next section for more details.) The current job is typically represented by a file object on top of the server loop. As the file is executed, other objects may be executed as well. For instance, a common occurrence is for a procedure to be defined and executed as in the following example (which is borrowed from *listing 2-3*):

```
%!PS-Adobe-2.0
/F { %def
        findfont exch scalefont setfont
} bind def
%%EndProlog
24 /Helvetica F
0 0 moveto
(Red Book) show
showpage
```

This program is represented by a file object on the execution stack that the scanner reads and interprets token by token. We have seen the execution of the scanner; now let's look at what happens when the procedure is executed.

When the **F** token is scanned and interpreted from the file object on top of the execution stack, it is seen to be an executable name. This name is looked up in the current dictionary stack, and an executable array (procedure body) is found. This procedure body is then pushed onto the execution stack:

{ findfont --exch-- --scalefont-- --setfont--}

-file-

{ --job server-- }

Remember that the array is represented by an array object, even when it is on the execution stack. *Figure 2.4* shows what this array object looks like on the execution stack.

The PostScript interpreter executes array objects one element at a time, leaving the unused part of the array on the execution stack. The interpreter always checks the remainder of the procedure body *before* it executes the first element. If the procedure body is empty, the interpreter discards it. This permits infinitely deep tail recursion, since the empty procedure bodies will not accumulate on the execution stack. (*Tail recursion* means that the recursive procedure call is the very last element (the tail) of the procedure body.)

figure 2.4

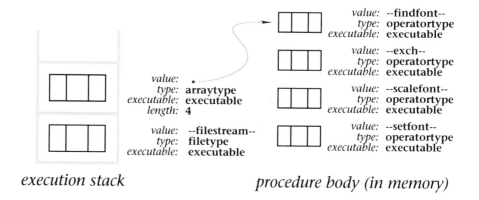

execution stack   *procedure body (in memory)*

2.9 THE SERVER LOOP

The execution stack starts out with a procedure that is an infinite loop. The interpreter is always busy executing this loop, even when the interpreter is in an idle state. This loop is known as the *server loop*, and each time around the loop it checks to see if there is a new job to execute (if one of the communications ports has become active). When a new job is discovered, a *file object* representing the standard input file is opened and placed on the execution stack. This file object is executed until the end-of-file indication is reached, at which point it is popped off the execution stack, and the interpreter reenters the server loop.

The primary task of the server loop is to isolate one batch job from another. Before each job starts, the server loop executes the **save** operator. When a job has finished executing, the server loop is re-entered, and a **restore** is performed, restoring the state of the interpreter back to exactly the state that was in effect at the start of the job.

Errors are caught by using the **stopped** operator. There is a discussion of this technique in Section 14.3.

In listing 2-5 is an idea of what the server loop looks like. A few pieces of pseudo-code are included to show some functionality without providing all the nuts and bolts. These are represented in **italics.** This example does not match any real server loop code, but it provides the theoretical model for how it operates. The server loop procedures for any given interpreter can be seen by simply executing this code: **128 array execstack ==**

listing 2-5 —————————————————————————————

```
/server save def          % save the initial state
{ %loop
      server restore          % when entering loop
      { %loop
         any port active { %if
               exit
         } if
      } loop   % until new job is encountered
      /server save def % before each job
      (%stdin) (r) file
      cvx stopped { % execute the file object
            errordict /handleerror get exec
            currentfile flushfile
      } if
} bind loop   % main server loop
```

—————————————————————————————————————

THE IMAGING MODEL

Painting isn't an æsthetic operation;
it's a form of magic designed as a mediator
between this strange hostile world and us....

– Pablo Picasso

3.1 INTRODUCTION

The PostScript language *imaging model* is the metaphor through which graphics are rendered on output devices. The imaging model consists of specific rules and mechanisms by which a picture is described, and its behavior is exactly predictable.

The imaging model for silk-screening, for example, might be loosely stated like this: "Ink is forced through a mask of film that adheres to a stretched piece of silk. Ink flows through the mask only where it has been cut away." The imaging model for the PostScript language might be stated: "Algorithmic paths are created to define an area or a series of lines, and ink is applied to those paths through one of several methods, including stroking, filling, halftoning, text rendering, and clipping."

In the world of computers, all graphics application programs have a graphic imaging model, whether it is explicitly stated or simply assumed. Even text editors have a paradigm for the lines of text being edited. Although video screens are two-dimensional, the model used by a drawing program may permit objects to overlap on the screen, as though there were a third dimension. There is no "correct" imaging model—it is just a consistent way of thinking about graphics that is useful to a computer program.

Writing a driver for an application to print through a PostScript interpreter is almost entirely the task of adapting one graphic imaging model to another. The act of printing a page is a translation of some computer graphics representation into a printed reality. If the software permits the user to draw a circle, for example, the circle must be stored in some way (the internal representation), and ultimately printed with whatever means are available.

3.2 APPLYING THE METAPHOR

The PostScript language uses a "path and paint" model for imaging. A *path* is constructed out of simple graphics primitives such as **moveto**, **lineto**, **curveto**, and **closepath**. The resulting path may then have *paint* applied to it with one of the *painting operators* (such as **fill** or **stroke**). Paint is opaque in the PostScript imaging model—that is, any color of paint will completely obscure any paint that may already have been laid on the page.

Path construction and painting operations in the PostScript language are *state-dependent*. All of the elements used in graphic operations are maintained by the PostScript interpreter in what is known as the *graphics state*. This includes the current path, the current line weight, the current color, the current transformation matrix, and other elements used in rendering graphics.

At any moment there is only one current path. The path can have additional elements added to it, it may be used by one of the painting operators, or it may even be initialized (with **newpath**). There can be many disconnected *subpaths* that together make up the current path.

The approach used for rendering graphics consists basically of the repetition of the following steps:

- Save the current state of the interpreter VM (memory).

- Establish a current point (with **moveto**).

- Construct a path, if needed (it is not necessary, for example, with **show**).

- Paint the path (or **show** characters), resulting in marks on the page.

- **restore** to the previously saved state.

- (Optional) Execute **showpage** to print the current page.

figure 3.1

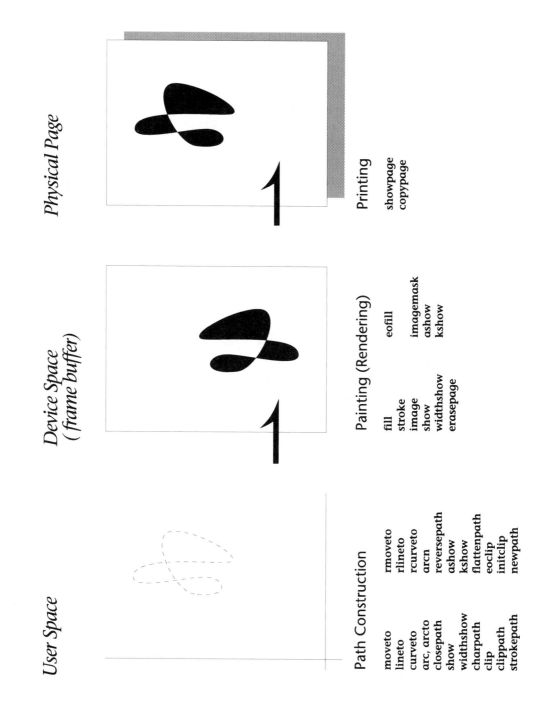

User Space

Device Space
(frame buffer)

Physical Page

Path Construction

moveto	rmoveto
lineto	rlineto
curveto	rcurveto
arc, arcto	arcn
closepath	reversepath
show	ashow
widthshow	kshow
charpath	flattenpath
clip	eoclip
clippath	initclip
strokepath	newpath

Painting (Rendering)

fill	eofill
stroke	imagemask
image	ashow
show	kshow
widthshow	
erasepage	

Printing

showpage
copypage

3.3 CONSTRUCTION OF PATHS

Paths are constructed using *path construction operators*. Here is a list of all of them:

moveto	lineto	curveto
rmoveto	rlineto	rcurveto
arc	arcn	arcto
closepath	clippath	charpath
clip	eoclip	reversepath
initclip	strokepath	flattenpath
show	widthshow	newpath
ashow	kshow	initgraphics
grestore	restore	grestoreall

Each of these adds to (or creates, or modifies) the current path. The **newpath**, **initgraphics**, **restore**, and **grestoreall** operators can be thought of as path construction operators, even though they are really path *destruction* operators. The variations on the **show** operator are path construction operators only in that they affect the current point, which is part of the current path.

The current path is part of the standard graphics state, and it is preserved (and restored or overwritten) by both the **gsave** and **grestore** operators and the **save** and **restore** operators.

The **clip** operator uses the current path (appending it to the current clip path) but does *not* destroy it. This is often the cause of strange program behavior when using **clip**. Using the **newpath** operator after the **clip** usually fixes these problems.

Construction of a path alone is not sufficient to cause marks to be made on the page. A path must be painted in order to see it.

THE GRAPHICS STATE AND PATHS

There is an interesting relationship between building the current path and changing the graphics state. For example, consider the short PostScript program given in *listing 3-1*. Notice that the constructed path has three elements: an initial **moveto** and two instances of **rlineto**, each of which appends a line segment to the current path. However, there are also three changes to the graphic state. The **setlinewidth** operator is invoked twice in this example, and **scale** is invoked once. What does this path look like on the final page, after it has been **stroke**d?

listing 3-1 ────────────────────────────────

```
%!PS-Adobe-2.0
%%Title: pathconstruct.ps
%%EndComments
/F { findfont exch scalefont setfont } bind def
%%EndProlog
 gsave
      400 300 moveto
      100 0 rlineto   % horizontal line
      2 setlinewidth
      4 4 scale
      0 100 rlineto   % vertical line
      1 setlinewidth
       gsave   % make the picture more interesting...
          14 /Times-Roman F (A) show
          2 -12 rmoveto -20 rotate (A) show
       grestore
      stroke
 grestore
 showpage
 %%Trailer
```

To answer this, one must look more carefully at the *graphics state* (and at *figure 3.2*). Here are the elements of the graphics state:

- **Current point and current path**
- **Current transformation matrix (CTM)**
- **Current font**
- Current color (or gray level)
- Line weight, line cap, and line join
- Line miter limit and dash pattern
- Current raster device
- Current clipping region
- All halftone parameters

The entries set in **bold** are the only elements of the graphics state that affect path construction directly. The others affect only the painting of the path. In *listing 3-1*, the **4 4 scale** *does* affect the subsequent execution of **rlineto**, causing the line to be (effectively) four times as long when it is appended to the current path. The path construction operators use the *current* transformation as the path is being constructed, but once an element of the current path exists, it is not affected by further changes to the coordinate system.

figure 3.2

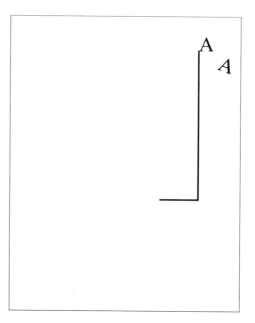

Another way to think of it is that changes to the current transformation matrix and the current font affect future elements of the path, but not existing elements.

Changes to the line width or the current color take effect only when **stroke** or **fill** is executed, and they apply to the entire current path.

3.4 PAINTING OPERATIONS

A path, once constructed, must be *painted* in order to make marks on the page. There are several painting operators, each of which causes some marks to be made in device space (assuming that some part of the path is within the clipping region, of course). Here is a list of painting operators:

fill	**eofill**	**stroke**
image	**imagemask**	
show	**widthshow**	
ashow	**kshow**	

When marks are made in device space by one of these painting operators, they stay there. Even the **showpage**, **erasepage**, and **framedevice** operators, which cause device space to be cleared, operate by painting the entire page with "white."

In the steps for path construction and painting outlined in Section 3.2, the use of **save** and **restore** guarantees the functional independence of each page element, although the marks on the page persist until **showpage** is finally executed.

3.5 WHAT HAPPENS TO THE CURRENT PATH?

There is only one current path in the graphics state. A large percentage of the execution of a document involves the construction and use of paths. It definitely helps to understand this mechanism and use it efficiently. In particular, keep the following in mind:

- It is inefficient to destroy a path explicitly (with **newpath**) if it will happen as a natural consequence of *using* the path (as it will with **stroke** or **fill**).

- Don't preserve the path (with **gsave** and **grestore**) if it isn't needed for anything.

It is unfortunately fairly common to see sequences like the following one in production software:

    0 0 moveto 100 100 lineto
    gsave stroke grestore newpath

The path is carefully preserved, stroked, and restored, only to be destroyed immediately with **newpath**. In this case three unnecessary operators are executed for every line drawn.

3.6 PROCEDURES FOR CONSTRUCTING PATHS

It is often found that the kinds of shapes rendered by a graphics application require a little more than simple calls to **lineto** or **curveto**. In these cases, after careful consideration, it may be determined that writing a *procedure* to implement a particular graphic primitive is advantageous. For example, rectangles, circles, arrowheads, and other shapes may be fundamental parts of your application.

It is important to construct efficient procedures. Defining a procedure and using it instead of a number of PostScript language commands is only a useful technique if the procedure is faster than the unrolled code would have been. There are a couple of considerations that make it easier to generate fast procedures:

- What is the least amount of critical data needed from the host application to construct the required shape?

- What is the natural order and format in which to supply the data, based on the PostScript operators to be used?

- How should the operands be presented on the operand stack to minimize the computation required of the procedure itself?

For example, if the **arc** operator is used (as it is to construct a circle), the center and radius should be specified, not the corners of a bounding rectangle (see Section 5.5 and Figure 5.1). If an arrowhead is to be drawn, it should be carefully worked into the line-drawing primitives like **lineto** and **curveto**, making use of the way paths are naturally constructed.

RECTANGLES

A common task performed by a graphics application is to draw a rectangle, often one that is shaded and/or outlined with a border. There are many ways to represent a rectangle. The goal, when writing a PostScript driver, is to minimize the computation required and the data transmitted. For example, if rectangles are always oriented either vertically or horizontally (never at an angle), they can be represented by two points (for example, the lower left and upper right corners), or by one corner and the *width* and *height* of the rectangle. However, if the rectangle may be rendered at an angle, *four* points are necessary, or two points and an angle (although that would require more computation).

A rectangle procedure may require several *painting attributes* (like a gray level and a line weight) as well as the geometric information to construct the rectangle. If so, this data should be passed to the procedure on the operand stack. *Listing 3-2* provides a good rectangle procedure.

listing 3-2 ────────────────────────────

```
%!PS-Adobe-2.0
%%Title: rectangle.ps
%%EndComments
% "R" takes the following arguments:
% lineweight linegray fillgray
% width height LLx LLy
/R { %def
    gsave
        moveto
        1 index 0 rlineto
        0 exch rlineto
        neg 0 rlineto
        closepath
        gsave setgray fill grestore
        setgray setlinewidth stroke
    grestore
} bind def
%%EndProlog
3 .5 .9 200 300 100 100 R
showpage
%%Trailer
```

────────────────────────────

This example draws a rectangle that is 200 points wide, 300 points tall, is filled with 10 percent gray (0.9) and stroked with a 3-point line at 50 percent gray (0.5). Notice that the procedure uses the values directly from the stack (rather than defining them into a dictionary and calling them up again), since they are only needed once.

CIRCLES AND ARCS

Circles are another simple graphic shape for which there are many, many possible representations. The PostScript language has one in the **arc** operator. To draw a circle in the PostScript language, use the method provided in the imaging model.

listing 3-3 ————————————————————————————————

```
%!PS-Adobe-2.0
%%Title: circle.ps
%%EndComments
% "C" takes the following arguments:
% linewidth linegray fillgray
% X Y r ang1 ang2
/C { %def
    gsave
        newpath 0 360 arc
        gsave setgray fill grestore
        setgray setlinewidth stroke
    grestore
} bind def
%%EndProlog
3 .5 .9 300 500 200 C
showpage
%%Trailer
```

Listing 3-3 draws a circle of radius 200 at the point 300, 500, fills it with 10 percent gray (0.9), and strokes it with a 3-point line at 50 percent gray.

ARROWHEADS

Lines terminating with arrow heads are commonplace in many graphics applications. In *listing 3-4* is a procedure that will draw an arrow head at the current point, at a specified orientation and line width. (The line width is used only as a size reference—the arrow head is scaled to an appropriate size for lines of the specified width.) The orientation is supplied by a *previous* point. The arrow head is drawn parallel to the line *implied by* the *previous* point and the *current* point, which should be the tangent of the line at the end point. See *Listing 3-4.*

listing 3-4 ────────────────────────────────

```
%!PS-Adobe-2.0
%%Title: arrowhead.ps
%%EndComments
%%BeginProcSet: arrows 1.0 0
% "arrowhead" takes these arguments:
% lineweight prevX prevY
/arrowhead { %def
    gsave
        currentpoint
        4 2 roll exch 4 -1 roll exch
        sub 3 1 roll sub
        exch atan rotate dup scale
        -1 2 rlineto
        7 -2 rlineto
        -7 -2 rlineto
        closepath fill
    grestore
    newpath
} bind def
/l^ { %def    % lineto-arrow
    currentlinewidth currentpoint 5 3 roll
    lineto
    currentpoint stroke moveto
    arrowhead
} bind def
/rl^ { %def    % rlineto-arrow
    currentlinewidth currentpoint 5 3 roll
    rlineto
    currentpoint stroke moveto
    arrowhead
} bind def
/arc^ { %def    % arc-arrow
    5 copy arc
    currentpoint stroke moveto          % stroke arc
% getting the correct orientation for the arrowhead
% is tricky. This procedure uses the arguments to
% "arc" to determine the tangent of the curve at the
% endpoint, and it orients the arrowhead along that
% tangent line.  It leaves an X-Y point that is just
% behind the arrowhead along the tangent.
```

```
% newX = X + radius * cos(endAngle-1)
% newY = Y + radius * sin(endAngle-1)
    exch pop 1 sub   % endAngle - 1 degree
    dup cos 2 index mul 4 index add      % arrowX
    exch sin 2 index mul 3 index add     % arrowY
    currentlinewidth 2 add 3 1 roll      % thickness
    arrowhead pop pop pop                % draw ->
} bind def
%%EndProcSet: arrows 1.0 0
%%EndProlog
%%Page: 1 1
% line sample:
200 600 moveto
0 10 360 {
    currentlinewidth .1 add setlinewidth
    gsave
    dup cos 100 mul
    exch sin 100 mul
    rl^
    grestore
} bind for
newpath
% curve sample:
/radius 10 def .1 setlinewidth
0 30 360 {
    /radius radius 10 add def
    280 230 radius 0 5 -1 roll arc^
} bind for
showpage
%%Trailer
```

Listing 3-4 contains a fairly sophisticated set of procedures. There is one procedure to draw an arrowhead at the current point, and there are three other procedures (**rl^**, **l^**, and **arc^**) that work like **rlineto**, **lineto**, and **arc**, respectively, except that each draws an arrowhead at the end of the line segment (or arc) using the **arrowhead** procedure. In the **arc^** procedure, the tangent to the curve is computed and a point is passed to the **arrowhead** procedure for orienting it properly. It is more likely that the host application would provide this simple *x-y* location to orient the arrowhead, to avoid this largely unnecessary calculation. There are also other possible orientation schemes.

Note:

*Keep track of the current path, and use it naturally.
Avoid unnecessary path operations or safeguards that
may seem at first like good, defensive programming.
The language is designed to work the way you probably
need it to work, and it is best to use it that way.*

The **fill**, **eofill**, and **stroke** operators effectively "use up" the current path, destroying it when they are through (by executing the equivalent of **newpath**). The **image** and **imagemask** operators do not disturb the current path in any way. The **show** operator and its siblings make changes only to the current point (corresponding to the width of the string being shown), and otherwise do not disturb the current path.

3.7 TEXT OPERATIONS

In the PostScript language, text is rendered with the **show** operator (or one of its relatives). The **show** operator is somewhat special in the PostScript imaging model, in that there are very specific requirements for setting text that may not apply when rendering other graphic elements.

In particular, text characters are normally set one after another, along a *baseline*. The **show** operator leaves the current point when it is done, rather than destroying the path as other path painting operators do. Furthermore, **show** requires not only a current point but a *current font* in order to render text (unlike other painting operators).

In order to effectively make use of the PostScript imaging model, one should understand just what effect the **show** operator has, and when it is appropriate, for instance, to use **gsave** and **grestore** to preserve the current point (and the current font).

Let us consider two variations that print a couple of lines of 10-point text (*listing 3-5*).

listing 3-5 —————————————————————

```
%!PS-Adobe-2.0
%%Title: text examples
%%EndComments
/F { findfont exch scalefont setfont } bind def
/S1 { moveto show } bind def

/S21 { moveto gsave show grestore } bind def
/S22 { %def
        0 exch rmoveto gsave show grestore
} bind def
%%EndProlog

% method 1:
10 /Times-Roman F
(method 1:) 72 512 S1
(Viva Nuestra Senora de Guadelupe!)  72 500 S1
(Viva la Independencia!) 72 488 S1

% method 2:
10 /Times-Roman F
(method 2:) 72 412 S21
( There was a young lady named Bright,) -12 S22
( Whose speed was far faster than light;) -12 S22
(    She set out one day) -12 S22
(    In a relative way) -12 S22
( And returned home the previous night.) -12 S22
(          -Arthur Buller) -12 S22
showpage
%%Trailer
```

The first method in *listing 3-5* (labeled *method 1* in the comments) has a very simple procedure (called **S1**) which does a **moveto** and a **show**. The *x,y* location for the text is passed on the stack along with the string, and the current font is understood already to exist. The second example (called *method 2*) uses a different approach. The first line uses an *x,y* pair, as does method 1, except that it uses **gsave** and **grestore** to preserve the current point after **show** is finished. Subsequent lines of text are set with just a relative quantity (an amount to move down before printing the line). This enables the driver to generate and transmit less data, but there is a greater computation cost in doing the **gsave**, **grestore**, **exch**, and **rmoveto** for each line.

The two examples above are inherently based on the behavior of the **show** operator: It always leaves the current point at an adjusted position (usually to the right of the text shown) based on the character widths. In method 2, the second line (and subsequent lines) of text are dependent on the first, in the sense that the position is relative to the first line.

Another approach might be to have a procedure for setting an entire paragraph, where the inter-line spacing is constant for the whole paragraph, and the **moveto** can be generated easily from within the code.

The rest of this book is dedicated to the decision-making process. The PostScript language execution and imaging models provide great freedom in setting text, but in any environment there are constraints or advantages that may dictate using one method over another. Understanding the workings of the mechanism will help you to make these decisions.

CHARACTER WIDTHS

Character widths are stored within PostScript language font programs as *displacements* in coordinate space. The best way to think of text setting is to view each character as an *origin*, a *shape*, and a *width*. The relationship between the shape and the origin is fixed—the origin is the 0,0 point in *character space* (described later) and the character draws itself relative to that location. The *width* is essentially an implicit **rmoveto** that occurs after the character shape is rendered. (See *figure 3.3*).

The character width is not related to the actual execution of the character shape (the shape may even be in the font cache, and not get executed at all). This is not important unless you are building font characters yourself. (See also Section 9.3). Remember that characters widths have both an x and a y component. A common bug is to call **stringwidth** but to forget that there are two values returned. Typically, the extra number stays on the stack until a **typecheck** occurs later.

figure 3.3

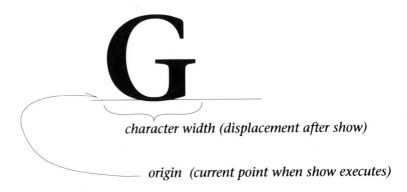

character width (displacement after show)

origin (current point when show executes)

The important thing to remember is to use the way the PostScript language renders text instead of fighting it. Below are some aspects of the execution and imaging models that commonly present difficulty. Each of these is a symptom of not having used the language effectively:

- When you try to use **save** and **restore** at the page boundaries, you discover that it destroys the current font at the bottom of the page, and it needs to be explicitly re-set at the beginning of the next page.

- You find that changing fonts in the middle of a line of text makes it hard to justify the line, since the character widths are different for the two fonts.

- You are using **stringwidth** to determine where text is going to be placed. (The application should always control placement of text, and should know the character widths beforehand.)

- When you relocate or remove graphics from a file, the text does not print in the correct position on the page, since it relies on the current point being in the right place.

chapter 3 THE IMAGING MODEL

Some thought is required to build a complex program, and using the PostScript language is no exception. Learning the characteristics of each text operator and remembering the semantics of the imaging model will help enormously in designing a simple and efficient program.

3.8   CLIPPING

Clipping is a mechanism used to limit the area in which paint can be applied by the PostScript language painting operators. It behaves like a stencil.

There is always a clipping path in the graphics state, which by default is the current page boundary. The clipping path may have further restrictions appended to it or removed from it (with **grestore**, for example)—but it can't be replaced entirely. The **clip** operator appends the current path to the current clipping path (but does *not* destroy the current path).

COMPLEXITY AND PERFORMANCE

Clipping requires computation. When the PostScript interpreter paints a path, it must determine whether or not the marks fall within the current clipping path. This computation can be quite expensive, depending upon the implementation. Additionally, the **clip** operator reduces the current path to a *flattened* path as it is added to the clipping path. This means that it is broken down into line segments. There is a practical limit on how many path elements may be stored, both in the clipping path and in the current path in the graphics state. Exceeding this limit will result in a **limitcheck** error. Depending on the path and the resolution of the output device, a flattened path may contain hundreds or even thousands of elements, and care must be exercised when using **clip**.

One source of unexpected behavior stems from the fact that the **clip** operator does not destroy the current path. Remember to execute **newpath** after **clip** unless the current path is to be used for something else. The **clip** operator does not initialize the current path.

3.9 RASTERIZATION

Rasterization is a term for the process of converting the original high-level PostScript language description into *rasters*, or plain old bits of black or white (or plain old 16 bits of color or plain old 8 bits of grayscale, or whatever is the appropriate fodder for the output device). In particular, rasterization is the end result of all the painting operators such as **stroke, fill,** and **show.**

The real device independence of the PostScript language lies in the fact that the interpreter performs the rasterization at the resolution of the output device. Only high-level descriptions of graphics are sent to the printer. (Even scanned images are scalable, and not resolution-dependent.)

In many devices, the PostScript interpreter can rasterize in parallel with the interpretation of the program, and may be deferred when the original painting operator is executed. This is especially true in high-speed printing devices, where some of the final rasterization may be done on the fly during **showpage.**

Most programs need not be concerned with the rasterization process itself—the purpose of the PostScript language is that the user program is removed from the level of rasterization to ensure true device independence.

3.10 **SAVE** AND **RESTORE**

The **save** and **restore** mechanism is a fundamental part of the PostScript imaging model. It affects all aspects of a program, including its execution, the graphics state, and its use of memory and resources. As a starting place for this discussion, here is a rule of thumb:

> *If you find it difficult to get **save** and **restore** to work correctly in your program, you should redesign your program.*

A PostScript program should be designed from the very start to work easily with the state-dependent execution model of the PostScript interpreter. Page elements should be independent of one another. Each page should be functionally independent of all others. (See Chapter 6). The graphics state stack should naturally parallel the execution of your program.

Simply stated, **save** and **restore** (they are always used in pairs) provide a mechanism for saving the current state of the world and then returning to it. This mechanism affects everything (except the contents of the stacks and the marks on the current page). It saves the contents of dictionaries, the current line weight, the current halftone screen, the current font, the path, the clipping region, the existence of string bodies, array objects, and all objects in memory.

There is nothing special required to use **save** and **restore** effectively. They should be designed in from the beginning into any procedures that use memory. If memory conservation is not an issue, **gsave** and **grestore** will probably work just as well, and are more efficient.

In general, every procedure that affects the graphics state in some way should contain either **gsave** and **grestore** or **save** and **restore**. Chapter 6 provides more detail on how to structure procedures and programs to take full advantage of these operators. Section 13.3 discusses the use of **save** and **restore** for memory management.

3.11   THE FONT CACHE

The *font cache* is an optimization technique. The best way to use the font caching mechanism is to be glad that it exists. There is no direct means for manipulating the font cache, and it is not intended for general use. However, it is useful to have some background on how it works.

Characters go into the font cache whenever they are executed by the **show** operator, as long as they will fit (based on the font caching limits currently in effect, not on how many characters are already in the cache) and as long as the font itself executes the **setcachedevice** operator (the only other choice is **setcharwidth**, which explicitly avoids the font cache).

Characters are removed from the font cache on a *least-recently-used* basis whenever the available space in the cache is exhausted. The font cache occupies a fixed amount of space in most implementations (although not all of them), and characters always are added to the cache if they qualify. If there is not enough room, the least recently used characters are removed.

Entries are made into the font cache for a single character, and are not pre-cached for an entire font. The entry is made based on the current font, the size and orientation of the character (based on the current transformation matrix), the character name, and its width.

chapter 4

EMULATORS AND TRANSLATORS

*Nature has ... some sort of
arithmetical-geometrical coordinate system,
because nature has all kinds of models.*

– *Richard Buckminster Fuller*

4.1 INTRODUCTION

The PostScript language can be thought of in two distinct ways: it provides an *imaging model* for describing and printing complex text and graphics, and it is a complete and general programming language.

A *printer emulator* is software that uses the PostScript programming language to implement some other imaging model. The simplest example of this might be a line printer emulator, in which the ASCII text sent to the printer is simply listed out on the page rather than being interpreted.

A *print format translator* is a host-based program which converts a file created for another printing device (and its accompanying imaging model) into a PostScript file. For instance, the program might take line printer input files and produce PostScript output files which may then be transmitted to a device for printing.

There are many problems which can arise in translating other print files or emulating other printers, most of which generally have to do with fonts. When setting text, the widths of the individual characters are very important in making decisions about line breaks and for centering text. If text has been formatted for a different printer (perhaps with different character widths for its fonts) the translation process becomes more difficult. In addition, many print files may have been decomposed from their original editable form into an output format appropriate for a particular printer, and what used to be text or labels might be vectors or bit images by the time the print file is produced. At that stage, there is no reasonable way to reverse-engineer the print file to produce the clean typography which the PostScript language provides.

Whenever possible, it is best to compose pages originally with PostScript devices in mind, and to use font width tables that correspond to the fonts that will be used on the PostScript printer. It is also best to consider the PostScript imaging model fully, and to adapt the editable representation to the PostScript language model when producing the print file, rather than translating it after the fact, or programming the interpreter to emulate another printer.

This chapter outlines some of the best methods for writing emulators and translators when it is not possible to modify the software which produces the print files. Chapter 5 is devoted to the subject of creating PostScript language page descriptions directly from the composing application.

4.2   EMULATING ANOTHER PRINTER

To successfully emulate another printer in the PostScript language, the software must be able to print any file that would produce results on the original printer. This means that any control sequences, condensed printing modes, or other features of the printer must be mimicked completely.

From an implementation point of view, an emulator is simply a program that executes in the printer and reads directly from the input (superseding the interpreter). As input is received, the emulator looks for control codes, keeps track of line positions, reproduces condensed or overstrike modes, and prints pages as required. Because the PostScript language is interpreted, the program loop is actually re-interpreted each time around, and must be written carefully in order to make performance reasonable.

Listing 4-1 is a simple loop that reads a fixed-length string from the current file (normally the standard input stream, **%stdin**) and prints it, quitting only when the **readstring** operator detects an end-of-file indication. Note that no parsing of the string is attempted, no control codes are recognized, and there is no capability to change fonts. In fact, with this example even line breaks (carriage return characters) are ignored.

listing 4-1 ────────────────────────────────

```
%!PS-Adobe-2.0
%%Title: emulate1
/buff 128 string def
/emulate1 { %def
    { %loop
        currentfile buff readstring
        exch show not { exit } if
    } loop
    showpage
} bind def
%%EndProlog
72 750 moveto
/Courier findfont 10 scalefont setfont
emulate1
So spake the Fiend, and with necessity,
The tyrants plea, excused his devilish deeds. -Milton
```

────────────────────────────────

The **readline** operator may be used to automatically recognize newline characters, but with even this simple change the program becomes much more complex. For instance, there is immediately the possibility of trying to read in a line that is longer than the allocated buffer size (this is not a problem with the **readstring** operator, since it does not look for newline characters, it simply fills the buffer). Additionally, depending on the communications channel, newlines may be handled differently in different environments and by different PostScript interpreters.

In the purest sense, it is better not to use **readline**, but instead to use **search** to parse for various escape sequences and newline characters explicitly. *Listing 4-2* is a revised form of the previous example. It searches for *linefeed* characters.

listing 4-2

```
%!PS-Adobe-2.0
%%Title: simple line printer emulator
/buff 5000 string def
/leftmargin 72 def  /topmargin 72 def
/bottom 72 def  /top 792 topmargin sub def
/ptsize 10 def /lead 10 def
/EOLchar (\n) def  % line feed
/F { findfont exch scalefont setfont } bind def
/newline { %def
    currentpoint exch pop lead sub
    dup bottom lt { %if
        showpage
        pop top
    } if
    leftmargin exch moveto
} bind def
/emulate { %def
    { %loop
        currentfile buff readstring exch
        EOLchar
        { %loop (innermost)
            search { %ifelse
                show newline
            }{ %else
                show exit
            } ifelse
        } loop
        not { %if readstring found EOF
            exit
        } if
    } loop
    showpage
    leftmargin top moveto
} bind def
%%EndProlog
%%BeginSetup
ptsize /Courier F
leftmargin top moveto
%%EndSetup
emulate
I wasted time, and now doth time waste me;
For now hath time made me his numbering clock;
My thoughts are minutes.
    - William Shakespeare
```

There are several items of note in this program. The innermost loop, for instance, takes advantage of the syntax of the **search** operator. After calling **search**, there is a boolean on the top of the operand stack which indicates the success or failure of the search. This boolean is used immediately by the **ifelse** statement, and one of the two procedure bodies is conditionally executed. If the search failed, the original string is still on the stack, and it is merely printed (**show**) and the loop is exited. If the search succeeded, there are *three* strings on the stack. The topmost one is the portion of the string just before the newline (the newline was the *match* string provided to **search**), which is then printed (with **show**). The remaining two strings are already in the correct position for another call to the **search** operator, so it is okay to just drop through the loop and re-enter at the top. The **search** operator was designed very carefully to return on the stack the information that is most likely to be needed, in an appropriate order, and it is easy to write a program that takes advantage of this design.

This use of **search** can easily be extended to search for other characters as well as the newline character, although the inner loop would become more complicated. For instance, the *tab* character could be caught, and perhaps the *escape* character, in order to interpret control sequences.

THE **STRINGWIDTH** OPERATOR

If the printer emulator is likely to be faced with printing text, be sure to read Chapter 7, which presents several approaches to setting text, including font changes, justification, leading, and underlining. In general, however, all text-setting algorithms (whether implemented in an emulator or in a print driver) need to know the widths of character strings in order to make positioning judgements. Widths are normally made available on the host system for computing line breaks, but an emulator is forced to do the calculations in the PostScript interpreter.

Character widths can be obtained using the **stringwidth** operator. This operator requires a current font (and a current point) and a string object on the operand stack. It returns *two* values, which represent the width of the string in both x and y. The *width* of a string is defined to be the distance by which the current point is modified if the given string were printed in the current font. Here is an example of its use (a session from an interactive PostScript interpreter):

```
PS> 0 0 moveto
PS> /Times-Roman findfont
PS> 12 scalefont setfont
PS> (TRANSLATING EXISTING FILE FORMATS)
PS> dup stringwidth exch == ==
230.316
0
PS>
```

The **stringwidth** operator can take almost as long to execute as **show**, since it does the same work of imaging the characters into the font cache and computing the offset to the current point that would occur. It is not too unreasonable to say that printing time *doubles* when the width of a string must be computed before it is printed. Although the characters are already in the font cache when **show** is executed, the overhead in interpretation and execution time required to compute the string's width and to adjust the current point tend to offset this.

Whenever possible, an emulator written in the PostScript language should avoid computing the width of a character string. For instance, if line breaks have already been determined (as is usually the case in line printer output) and the text is not justified, there is no reason to measure the string.

TEXT JUSTIFICATION IN AN EMULATOR

Performing full justification on a line of text with more than one font presents some tough problems for an emulator. First the line of text must be collected, and each substring (per font used) must be measured with **stringwidth**. Then the number of *spaces* must be counted, as well as the total number of characters in the line. Finally a subtraction and division problem are performed to figure out how much the line must be stretched to fit the margins, and the error divided evenly among the spaces or characters in the string and **widthshow** (or **ashow**) is called.

The program in *listing 4-3* is a printer emulator. It emulates a fictitious printer that is reasonably close to several real-world printers. It takes ASCII input data already broken into lines (it uses **readline**, in fact) and prints it with a variety of possible fonts. It is designed to use a default font (which you can specify) and to search for any of several *escape sequences* which permit changing fonts and going into or out of "justification" mode. The following are the recognized escape sequences:

ESC Sequence	Function	Result
ESC **Y**	justification on	
ESC **N**	justification off	
ESC **0**	set font 0	(roman)
ESC **1**	set font 1	(bold)
ESC **2**	set font 2	(italic)
ESC **3**	set font 3	(bold italic)

The escape character and the individual commands are "soft." The fonts mapped to the font codes are also soft. The **0**, **1**, **2**, and **3** in the font codes are, in this example, actually the ASCII versions of those numbers (48, 49, and so on) so that the example program is readable. Similarly, the escape character is set to the caret character (^). In a real emulator, these would probably be changed. This emulator prints at roughly 17 pages per minute on current implementations, with a good mix of fonts and in full justification mode.

listing 4-3

```
%!PS-Adobe-2.0
%%Title: justify.ps
%%Creator: Glenn Reid
%%EndComments
%%BeginProcSet: general 1.0 0
/FS { findfont exch scalefont } bind def
%%EndProcSet: general 1.0 0

%%BeginProcSet: justify 1.0 0
/spacecount { %def
    0 exch
    (\040) { %loop   (space)
        search { %ifelse
            pop 3 -1 roll 1 add 3 1 roll
        }{ pop exit } ifelse
    } loop
} bind def
/justify { %def   % mark (text) <font> (text) <font>
    /spaces 0 def
    /currentwidth 0 def
    /currlength 0 def
    counttomark /num exch def
    2 2 num { %for  % roll through stack and count
        -2 roll setfont
        dup spacecount spaces add
        /spaces exch def
        dup stringwidth pop currentwidth add
        /currentwidth exch def
        dup length currlength add
        /currlength exch def
        currentfont
    } for
    currlength 1 le { setfont show } { %ifelse
        /adjust %def
            columnwidth currentwidth sub
            spaces 0 eq { %ifelse
                currlength 1 sub
            }{ %else
                spaces
            } ifelse div
        def
        num 2 idiv %repeat
            spaces 0 eq { %ifelse
                { %repeat
                    setfont adjust 0 3 -1 roll ashow
                }
            }{ %else
```

```
                    { %repeat
                        setfont adjust 0 32 4 -1 roll
                        widthshow
                    }
                } ifelse
            repeat
        } ifelse
    } bind def
%%EndProcSet: justify 1.0 0

%%BeginProcSet: linemulator 1.1 0
/buff 1000 string def   % longest line for "readline"

% for recognizing escape sequences to change fonts
% and enter/leave "justify" mode:
/ESC (^) def  % escape character
/justON (Y) 0 get def % ESC-Y
/justOFF (N) 0 get def % ESC-N
/QUIT (Q) 0 get def       % ESC-Q
/zero (0) 0 get def        % for subtracting ASCII offset
/newline { %def
    currentpoint exch pop lead sub
    dup bottom lt { %if
        showpage pop top
    } if
    leftmargin exch moveto
} bind def
/linetoolong { %def
    newline (%%[Error: line too long.]%%) show
    showpage
} bind def
/printline { %def
    JUST { %ifelse
        counttomark 2 ge { justify } if
    }{
        counttomark 1 ge { show } if
    } ifelse
    newline
} bind def
/emulate { %def
% read currentfile one line at a time.  Search for
% ESC sequences. If not found, just "show" with
% current font and move on.  If justification is
% turned on, then LEAVE all the strings and the
% correct font dictionaries on the stack, and call
% "justify" at the end of the line:
    /fmax fonts length def
    /top 792 topmargin sub def
    /JUST justification def
    leftmargin top moveto
```

```
/sv save def
{ %loop
    mark currentfile buff { readline } stopped {
        linetoolong stop
    } if
    not /done exch def % use the boolean later
    { %loop      % handle escape sequences
        ESC search { %ifelse
            JUST { %ifelse
                exch pop exch currentfont exch
            } {
                show pop
            } ifelse
            dup length 0 eq {
                pop ESC JUST { %ifelse
                    exch currentfont exch
                } if
                printline exit
            } if
            dup 0 get  % escape argument
            true exch % look for ESC-fontchange?
            dup justON eq   {
                /JUST true def exch pop
                false exch
            } if
            dup justOFF eq  {
                /JUST false def exch pop
                false exch
            } if
            dup QUIT eq { /done true def exit } if
            exch { %ifelse
                zero sub % subtract ASCII offset
                dup dup fmax le
                exch 0 ge and { %ifelse
                    fonts exch get setfont
                    dup length 1 sub
                    1 exch getinterval
                }{ %else
                    pop ESC JUST { %ifelse
                        exch currentfont exch
                    }{
                        show
                    } ifelse
                } ifelse
            }{ %else
                pop
                dup length 1 sub
                1 exch getinterval
            } ifelse
        }{ %else
```

```
JUST { %ifelse
    dup length 0 ne { %ifelse
        currentfont printline
    }{ pop printline } ifelse
}{ %else
    dup length 0 ne { %ifelse
        printline
    }{ %else
        pop newline
    } ifelse
} ifelse exit
        } ifelse
    } loop
    cleartomark
    done { exit } if
    currentpoint
    /JUST JUST
        sv restore /sv save def
    def moveto
    } loop
    showpage
    sv restore
} bind def
%%EndProcSet: linemulator 1.1 0
%%EndProlog
%%BeginSetup
/columnwidth 432 def
/justification false def
/leftmargin 108 def
/topmargin 72 def
/bottom 72 def
/lead 14 def
/fonts [ %def
    12 /Times-Roman FS  % ESC-0
    12 /Times-Bold FS      % ESC-1
    12 /Times-Italic FS    % ESC-2
    12 /Times-BoldItalic FS % ESC-3
] def
fonts 0 get setfont
%%EndSetup
emulate
(turn on justification after this line)^Y
Here is ^1bold^0, here is ^2italic^0, and here is
^3BoldItalic^0.
^NNo other justification is necessary.^Q
```

4.3   TRANSLATING EXISTING FILE FORMATS

A description of how to write a print format translator is not directly within the scope of this book, since it most often means writing an application on a host computer to accomplish the translation. However, the PostScript language output which is produced by the translator should be designed carefully, and there are several issues that are likely to be common to many different kinds of translators.

UNITS

One of the first issues that must be addressed when translating a print file intended for another printer is to determine what units or measurements were used in the original file, and to convert or scale them into an appropriate PostScript coordinate system.

Conversion between number systems can result in significant round-off error in computation. When setting text and producing graphics, exact tolerances are needed to preserve the quality of the page image. It is best to study the relationship between the host units used by the host application and the default PostScript coordinate system and to perform the simplest possible conversion.

One way to map an application's coordinate system into the units that the PostScript language uses is simply to use the **scale** operator. However, the following issues should be considered if this technique is chosen:

- Fonts are scaled separately from the user coordinate system, but they are rendered through the current transformation matrix. If the user-space transformation is modified, then the numbers provided to **scalefont** must be adjusted accordingly.

- The implicit mapping performed by the current transformation matrix represents a calculation. This calculation is performed whether or not the mapping is used as a means to reconcile coordinate system differences; taking advantage of this mechanism is essentially free.

- **showpage** performs an implicit **initgraphics**. It will be necessary to use **gsave** and **grestore** to preserve the coordinate system across pages, or to set it explicitly for each page.

For example, if the base coordinate system in a layout application uses *inches* as its unit of measurement, it is much more efficient to scale the PostScript coordinate system to match this than it is to programmatically convert numbers into points:

```
/in. { 72 mul } def
1 in. 2 in. moveto
```

This requires three name lookups, the execution of a procedure body, and two multiplication operations (as well as 6 more bytes of information to be received and parsed by the PostScript interpreter) to position the current point. Compare this to the following bit of code, which has the same function and more than twice as fast:

```
72 72 scale
1 2 moveto
```

FONTS

The most basic problem encountered in translating other print formats into the PostScript language is incompatibility among font libraries. If a fixed-pitch font is used (one in which all character widths are the same) the problem is simplified quite a bit, but in most cases involving proportional fonts, there will be incompatibilities. Deciding on a philosophical approach to these kinds of differences is perhaps the most difficult part of writing a good emulator or translator.

4.4 FONT DIFFERENCES

For both emulators and translators, it is a tough problem to print a document that was formatted for a different printer. Most formatting and typesetting decisions contain very typeface-specific assumptions. Line layout, justification, centering, and amount of text on a page are all contingent upon the fonts for which the document was originally formatted.

When the fonts available on the original printer do not match the fonts available on the PostScript device in question, the first step is to introduce a *font substitution* strategy. Essentially, a table is built that maps the generic Roman font to Times-Roman on the PostScript printer, and so on for all the possible fonts. Some of these substitutions will be better than others (depending on the similarities or differences between the original and substituted fonts), but they provide a good starting point. A refinement to this approach is to define additional fonts in the PostScript language that may more closely match the fonts on the original printer, rather than trying to use the existing PostScript fonts. In either case, when a font is encountered in the original print file, some PostScript font must be used.

At the second level, a decision must reached as to where compromises can be made. For instance, for text which is not justified, it may be best to allow the normal letter spacing of the PostScript font to prevail, as long as the lines will be approximately the correct length. However, with justified text (like the text you are reading, with the margins aligned on both sides) the difference in line lengths between the original line of text (set in one font) and the line set in Times-Roman on a PostScript printer must be accounted for.

The **widthshow** and **awidthshow** operators can be used to "stretch" a line of text to any arbitrary size, although the result may not necessarily look like the original text. Typographers usually prefer to modify the word spacing rather than the letter spacing (this means using **widthshow** and stretching only the space character). If the text is not justified, then the line can simply be printed with **show** and the result can be quite good, depending on the match of the substituted font. (Frequently the results are much better than the original printer may have been able to produce, if the font style is not particularly important.)

When the decisions have been made as to roughly how to deal with the original imaging model and font library, there are implementation decisions to be made. For printing text, switching from one font to another tends to be the most difficult task, especially when the text is justified. Depending on the information provided in the original print file, there are two schools of thought:

- Print all instances of any given font at once, for any particular page, regardless of their positions on the page.

- Proceed left to right, top to bottom, switching fonts as necessary.

If the print format you are translating has location information for each word (or letter, or string) independently, the first approach may be preferable, especially if there are many font changes. If the existing print format relies on the current position of one piece of text in order to set the next, this is probably not feasible. Sometimes this kind of positioning information can be computed from the original print file, even if it is not inherent in the original format.

For instance, the positions of the lines of text (or words of text, given many font changes) must be determined at some point in order to print them. Unfortunately, they are often computed in the printer simply because it seems easier. However, by keeping a width table for all characters of a font, it is fairly easy to compute the position of any word on a page simply by adding together the character widths of preceding characters. The resulting PostScript program can be enough faster to make the first of these approaches worth considering when the translator is being designed.

4.5 USING THE IMAGING MODEL

To translate a graphics data file into a PostScript print file, it is necessary to correctly translate all aspects of the graphic imaging model used by the original creator software. Whenever graphic print files are produced, assumptions are made about the capabilities of the output device and the semantics of the individual graphic objects (for example, the notion of an object being a circle, not just a series of vectors). Whenever these semantics can be preserved at a high level, the resulting PostScript program is more efficient (and the results are usually better).

PRESERVING HIGH-LEVEL INFORMATION

If the captions on an illustration or other text matter are pre-served as character information in the print file, the strings can be passed directly to the printer and set as text. However, if the text was reduced to a graphic representation such as vectors or pixels as the print file was produced, the semantic notion of text is lost. Similarly, if a line of text in the print file is originally set justified, it means that some computation was made to deter-mine where the words would be placed. If a print file translator can determine that all the words on the line are evenly spaced and were intended to be set justified, an invocation of **widthshow** may be generated for the entire line of text, rather than many instances of **moveto** and **show**. This would result in a significant performance gain.

RENDERING

The physical properties of a display or marking device heavily influence the way in which graphics are rendered. PostScript interpreters are currently designed to drive raster devices. In particular, the final page image is typically represented as a large pixel array. Other devices, notably pen plotters or vector dis-plays, may require an input file containing only the equivalent of **moveto** and **lineto** operations. The capabilities of the target device often factor heavily into the graphic imaging assump-tions in the print file.

For further discussion on adapting to the PostScript imaging model, read Chapter 3.

4.6   OPTIMIZING TRANSLATOR OUTPUT

There are several areas where the code produced by a translator can be optimized. As an example, consider a print file intended for a *pen plotter* which is restricted in movement along one axis at a time. It is common to see sequences like the following for positioning the pen in a plotting device:

```
0 150 rmoveto
300 0 rmoveto
```

This represents movement first in the y direction, then in the x direction. By recognizing this sequence in the original print file, it can easily be optimized by combining the motion into a single command:

300 150 rmoveto

This is quite a bit shorter than the original, and it will therefore transmit faster and be interpreted faster. The key is to recognize sequences or patterns in the original file that might be represented more compactly in the PostScript language.

Another important optimization relates to setting text. Strings should be printed in as long a chunk as is practical; entire lines at a time are best. As an example, consider two approaches to setting a line of text in which the word spacing needs to be modified slightly, as in the following example:

```
% first example:
0 800 moveto (Entire) show
4 0 rmoveto (line) show
4 0 rmoveto (at) show
4 0 rmoveto (a) show
4 0 rmoveto (time.) show
% second example:
0 800 moveto
4 0 32 (Entire line at a time) widthshow
```

Even if the first of these is optimized by putting the **rmoveto** operation into a short procedure, it is still much slower to reposition between words than to print the whole line, modifying the width of the space using **widthshow**, as is done in the second part of the example.

Chapter 7 contains more detailed information on text setting algorithms.

4.7 COMPUTATION AND DECISION-MAKING

In general, the goal when writing a PostScript language driver is to distill out as much computation as possible from the PostScript program. The PostScript language is extremely flexible, but it is designed as a final-form output representation, not as a layout or computation tool.

Making decisions at the PostScript interpreter level can also be quite expensive. As usual, it is best to make the decisions on the host computer if possible. Consider the mechanism presented in *listing 4-4* for performing line wrapping. This is not a recommended approach, given the amount of computation performed.

listing 4-4 ──────────────────────────────

```
%!PS-Adobe-2.0
%%Title: example of what not to do
/SH { %def
        dup stringwidth pop
        currentpoint 3 1 roll
        add 300 gt { %if
                72 exch 48 sub dup 36 lt { %if
                        showpage
                        pop 700
                } if
                moveto
        }{ %else
                pop
        } ifelse
        show
} bind def
%%EndProlog
72 700 moveto
/Times-Roman findfont 48 scalefont setfont
(As ) SH (usual, ) SH (it ) SH (is ) SH
(best ) SH (to ) SH (make ) SH (the ) SH
(decisions ) SH (on ) SH (the ) SH
(host ) SH (computer ) SH (if ) SH
(possible.) SH
showpage
%%Trailer
```

This program takes input text one word at a time and places each string on the page. Right before printing each word, its width is computed and added to the current point on the page. If the resulting position would exceed the right margin, that word is moved to the next line. If that new line is below the bottom margin (**36**), then **showpage** is first executed for the current page, and the current point is then moved to the top of the next page. There is a great deal of computation involved in doing this, and it may cause a PostScript printer to run at less than one fourth the speed which it might otherwise achieve if the same page were composed carefully on the host system.

chapter 5

DESIGNING THE PAGE
AND THE PROGRAM

*Computers are at a double disadvantage in
the production of documents. They are not clever,
like secretaries, nor can they read penciled
proofreader's marks, like typographers.*

– Brian K. Reid

5.1   INTRODUCTION

An important aspect of designing printer driver software is to
adapt the application's graphic data structures to the PostScript
language imaging model. If the application has a representation
for text, exactly how is it maintained? How are graphics edited,
stored, and represented? What might be the relationship
between filled regions in the PostScript language and the graphic texturing in the application's own representation?

As is the case with any output device, these internal graphic
imaging models must be translated into a format appropriate for
the printer: the PostScript language. The subject of this chapter
is the task of designing the page description as a software application in its own right.

5.2   PAGE LAYOUT CONSIDERATIONS

One of the basic ideas in the PostScript language model is the
coordinate system. It is best to think in terms of user space, and
not about the actual paper—the job of getting a piece of paper
under the coordinate system for printing is almost the last consideration, and the PostScript language is infinitely flexible
about the exact mapping of the user coordinate system onto the
physical paper.

Frequently, one of the first questions that arises in the early stages of laying out a PostScript language driver is: "Where is the top of the page?" Many imaging models work from the top of the page with positive *y* coordinates growing downward, rather than using the lower left corner as the origin. The way to think about this in the PostScript imaging model is to answer: "There is no page at the composition stage, only an infinite real number coordinate system."

A good way to think about page composition is to imagine the desired page at any size: 11 inches by 18 inches, 36 inches by 48 inches, or 8-1/2 inches by 11 inches, it doesn't matter. What matters is the relative positioning of page elements, the overall proportions of the page, and its design. The page can easily be scaled to print at any size and orientation, and on any kind of paper (or on many sheets instead of one) without much trouble. It is most important to consider how the page elements will interact with one another.

In fact, the individual page elements should probably interact very little. That is, each *page element* should be self-contained, and be placed and executed individually. Columns of text (or perhaps even individual lines of text) might be considered to be independent page elements. In this context, independent means that there should be no "ripple effects" from, say, changing the location of one page element, or selecting a thicker line weight or a different font. This kind of context should be isolated from one page element to another.

PAGE NESTING AND INDEPENDENCE

It is important that all of the individual page descriptions within a document print file maintain *functional independence* from one another. This means, informally, that you should not define a procedure in the midst of page 1 and then use it again on page 2. It also means that there should be *contextual independence* between the pages. There should be no leftover graphics state, no reliance on the contents of a variable that may have been defined on a previous page, and no carry-over of the current font. The motivations for this are many. Most important among them are the ability to reverse the pages for printing, and the ability to print pages in parallel. There is a much fuller coverage of this in Chapter 6, but it is mentioned here because it affects page layout design directly.

All programs in the PostScript language should be written as if they were *subroutines* rather than the main program. You should avoid PostScript language operators which are *absolute* (for instance, **initgraphics**, **grestoreall**, **defaultmatrix**, and so on). For example, a document that is composed to print on standard letter-sized paper should be written in such a way that it can easily be printed 2-up (two half-size page images on a single sheet of paper, side by side). In order to accomplish this, the coordinate system must be scaled to half its original size. If the document executes **initgraphics**, this effect is nullified, since the default transformation matrix is installed. Even simply printing a page in "landscape" mode will not work if the file contains a call to **initgraphics** or **grestoreall**. There is further discussion of this in Chapter 6.

Note:

> *Never initialize or replace the existing state of the interpreter. All changes should be modifications to the existing state, including changes to the transformation matrix, the halftone mechanism, the transfer function, and redefinitions for operator names. Always concatenate the new procedures or matrices with the existing ones.*

5.3 PRODUCING POSTSCRIPT LANGUAGE OUTPUT

The fundamental level of a PostScript driver is the "print statements" in the host application which actually emit code fragments. This level is often overlooked in the overall design of a PostScript driver, but it is an extremely important area to consider, especially in terms of efficiency. It is at this level that the basic translation from the application's internal data structures to the PostScript print format takes place. It is an important place to consider some of the higher-level concerns:

- Analyze the geometry or properties of the object being generated, and how it relates to the inherent PostScript imaging model.

- Identify the aspects of this page element that can be considered data, and the order in which these data are needed at the PostScript level.

- Perform any calculations necessary to convert data from the program's internal representation into the desired PostScript language representation.

- Decide whether to generate native PostScript code at this stage, or to generate a procedure call to a procedure defined in the prologue.

The machine-generated part of the data stream (the script) should be as compact, modular, and efficient as possible. The script segment of a PostScript program is tightly linked to procedure definitions in the prologue, and a large part of the design process for a PostScript language program is to decide what the distribution of labor should be between the prologue and the script.

Note:

Remember that the PostScript language is interpreted, and that it is a programming language only as one aspect of its design. It is best not to defer calculation (such as division problems, computing the diameter of a circle, or figuring the length of some text) to the interpreter. Instead, perform these calculations on the host system as the script is being generated, providing the data to the procedures in the format expected by the PostScript language and the individual operators used.

5.4 ROUND-OFF AND COORDINATE SYSTEMS

Raster output devices are digital. That is, the pixels that make up device space are discrete, and you either hit one of them or you don't. The user space coordinate system in the PostScript language model, however, is a real number coordinate system, based on the printer's point (1/72 of an inch). This permits very accurate construction of paths, since the paths are maintained as points in an ideal coordinate space. When the paths are painted, the decision is made as to which of the pixels should be painted.

Essentially, there are two possible approaches in a digital device such as a laser printer:

1. A **moveto** or **lineto** instruction falls on the nearest pixel boundary in device space.

2. A path operation (like **moveto**) is maintained as a real number.

Either of these methods could be adopted. The first method would help ensure uniformity of line weights, for example, but it would prove far less accurate for constructing curves and other complex shapes (especially character descriptions in fonts). The second method is the one chosen for the PostScript language. One side effect of this model is that stroked lines (or filled shapes) may vary by as much as one device pixel, depending on where the paths fall in device space. There is an easy way to coerce the path construction operators into behaving like the first example, if desired. (See Section 9.3.)

Be careful not to make any assumptions about the resolution or orientation of device space when you use the PostScript language, or your program may not be device-independent.

5.5 EFFICIENCY

The overall efficiency of a PostScript program is affected primarily by the following three factors:

1. Data transmission (and tokenizing) time

2. Computation overhead

3. Interpretation time

All three of these are of roughly equal importance, although one or the other of them may become more significant in a particular application or environment. For instance, at low baud rates across a serial connection, data transmission time is likely to be the primary bottleneck, whereas across a high bandwidth connection, it is often less significant. However, reducing the time the scanner takes to tokenize the input stream is beneficial at any data transfer rate.

DATA TRANSMISSION OVERHEAD

Transmission and tokenization overhead can be minimized by defining very short procedure names for use in the script section of the document (which is usually the largest part of any PostScript file). Avoiding the retransmission of redundant information can also play a large role (for instance, long font names or extra unnecessary **moveto** instructions).

Aside from the time it takes to transmit the data to the PostScript device, the scan time is proportional to the number of bytes in the data stream. Short identifiers can be scanned more quickly than long ones. Compare the following two PostScript language fragments:

```
%!PS-Adobe-2.0
%%EndProlog
gsave
 10 10 moveto
 20 10 lineto
 20 20 lineto
 10 20 lineto
 closepath fill
grestore
showpage
%%Trailer
```

```
%!PS-Adobe-2.0
/gs /gsave load def  /gr /grestore load def
/m /moveto load def
/l /lineto load def
/cf { closepath setgray fill } bind def
/S /showpage load def
%%EndProlog
gs
 10 10 m
 20 10 l
 20 20 l
 10 20 l
 0.5 cf
gr S
%%Trailer
```

chapter 5 DESIGNING THE PAGE AND THE PROGRAM

The second example is actually longer than the first, but the initial procedure definitions (the prologue) are only executed once. For a very short document like this, the first example is faster. However, it would not take very many more boxes to change the balance in favor of the second example, since the amount of information transmitted and scanned for each box is minimized.

Notice that, in the previous example, each time a box is drawn a very predictable data stream is produced. In particular, there is always the sequence of **moveto lineto lineto lineto closepath fill**. An extremely useful approach in program design is to look for patterns like this and to factor out repeated procedure calls from the script. The following fragment defines a procedure called **B** that combines the functions of **m**, **l**, and **cf** in the previous example:

```
%!PS-Adobe-2.0
/B { %def
    gsave
        moveto lineto lineto lineto
        closepath setgray fill
    grestore
} bind def
/S /showpage load def
%%EndProlog
0.5 10 10 20 10 20 20 10 20  B
S
%%Trailer
```

COMPUTATION

Consider the following illustration of computation overhead. The task at hand is to draw an arc of a circle, but the stored representation for this arc maintained by the composition software is much different than the model used by the native **arc** operator in the PostScript language. In the original representation, an arc is represented by storing two corners of the *bounding rectangle* of the arc, and two *angles* representing the starting and ending points for the arc. (See *figure 5.1*).

figure 5.1

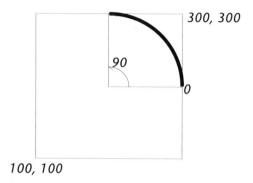

100, 100

The arc is stored in the host application simply as these six integers This representation must be converted to the syntax required by the **arc** operator, which uses the center of the arc, its radius, and the beginning and ending angles to represent the arc segment. *Listing 5-1* is a procedure that draws this arc merely by passing in the original six numbers as parameters. Incidentally, this listing is presented as an example of what it is best *not* to do.

listing 5-1 _____

```
%! example of how not to draw an arc:
/origmtx matrix def
/drawarc { %def
    /EndAngle exch def
    /StartAngle exch def
    /URy exch def
    /URx exch def
    /LLy exch def
    /LLx exch def
    gsave
        LLx URx add 2 div
        LLy URy add 2 div translate
```

chapter 5 DESIGNING THE PAGE AND THE PROGRAM

```
            newpath
            URx LLx sub
            URy LLy sub
            origmtx currentmatrix
                3 1 roll scale
                newpath
                0 0 0.5 StartAngle EndAngle arc
            setmatrix stroke
        grestore
    } bind def
    % end of prologue

    100 100 300 300 0 90 drawarc
    35 10 translate
    % as opposed to this:
    300 200 100 0 90 arc stroke
    showpage
```

Contrast this to a simple call to the built-in PostScript **arc** operator, without any of the attendant computation. The resulting
mark on the page is the same:

300 200 100 0 90 arc stroke

Refer to Section 3.6 for a good procedure to construct and paint
a circle with the **arc** operator.

INTERPRETATION TIME

Interpretation time is the time spent in the PostScript interpreter when no work is being done directly. For example, the
scan time, stack manipulations and name lookup required to
execute **0 0 moveto** are interpretation time necessary for establishing a current point.

Minimizing interpretation time is probably the most effective
way to improve the performance of a PostScript program. The
shorter the procedure is, and the fewer PostScript operators
executed, the more efficient the program will be. This can make
an order of magnitude difference in execution time under some
circumstances, given the interpreted nature of the language.

There are several ways to go about improving your PostScript program's efficiency, especially the interpreter overhead:

- *Study the listings in this book.* The examples throughout the text have been carefully designed to be efficient. Look carefully at the balance between the *data* passed in the script and the *procedures* defined in the prologue.

- *Study your script.* After you have gotten your program working, take a critical look at the script. Forget the constraints that you are working under, and forget the prologue procedures themselves. Are there any patterns in the output? Can you factor anything out of the script? There are many clues to the performance of your driver locked up in the script for an average document.

- *Look at your prologue procedures.* As a rule of thumb, if they are more than a few lines long, they are too complicated. If there are more than four or five instances of **roll**, **dup**, **exch**, or **index**, you may want to look more carefully at the data itself. Can it be rearranged? Can a division be performed by the host application? On the other hand, if there are a lot of instances of /**variable exch def**, look carefully to see if these dictionary entries need to be made. If the data is completely used up by the procedure, there is usually no reason to store the data in a dictionary, and it tends to be much slower to do so.

- *Do a timing test.* It is an extremely rare page that should take more than about five seconds to print. Without exception. This is true even when writing emulators. If your PostScript program is taking longer than that to print a page with text and graphics on it, start simplifying things. The **usertime** operator can be used for precise timings.

- *Implement special cases.* For the most part, procedures that are generalized to handle several possibilities are a bad idea in PostScript programming. It is better to make several simple, slightly different variations and invoke the appropriate one.

chapter 6

PROGRAM STRUCTURE

*Anything that's designed to do more than
one thing can't do any of them well.*

– Anonymous

6.1 INTRODUCTION

A PostScript language program contains several levels of structure. The program file conventionally consists of a *prologue*, a *script*, and a *trailer*. The prologue may be composed of several *procedure sets*, each of which is an independent package of procedures appropriate for a specific task. The script is divided into *pages*, and each page may contain many *page elements*. Within the execution of page elements, there are many procedure calls, and there is a structured interaction between these procedures and the PostScript language operators. The trailer section often is empty, but it can be used to restore the environment to its original state at the end of a document.

The program structure is important for several reasons. First, the structure affects the execution, as is true with most programming languages. The performance and robustness of the program are, in turn, linked to its execution. PostScript files also should be well-formed, according to specific structuring conventions (see Section 6.4) to cooperate effectively with print spoolers, page reversal programs, and applications wishing to import PostScript files as illustrations. There is a thorough discussion in Chapter 11 of the issues of embedding a complete PostScript document file within another PostScript file.

6.2 THE PROLOGUE AND SCRIPT MODEL

A good model of organization for a PostScript file is to divide it into two basic pieces, known as the *prologue* and the *script*. The *prologue* consists of procedure definitions and constants, and should contain only definitions (it should not, for instance, contain any modifications to the graphics state). The *script* is program-generated data along with procedure invocations (calls either to native PostScript language operators or to procedures defined in the prologue).

A software developer typically writes the prologue by hand, but the script is generated by software and is usually different for each document printed. The PostScript interpreter does not *require* the clean break in functionality found in the prologue-and-script model, but it is easier to maintain the software, and, more importantly, many kinds of pre- or post-processing of PostScript files depend on this structure. For instance, if the script can be broken cleanly into pages then host software can reverse the pages even after the application has produced a final print file. (See Section 6.3, MODULARITY AND PAGE STRUCTURE.)

Here is a simple example of a simple program written in the PostScript language that has an inherent prologue and script:

```
/F {
      findfont exch scalefont setfont
} bind def

12 /Optima-Oblique F
10 10 moveto
(Fairly Oblique) show
showpage
```

There is only a single procedure definition (the **F** procedure), and it must, of course, be defined before it can be executed. It is significant, however, that the definition precedes all of the executable code. For instance, if the **10 10 moveto** were performed first, the file would still execute correctly, but the clean distinction between the prologue definitions and the executable script would be lost.

What follows is the same program with PostScript language comments included to indicate the structure of the file. These are known as *structure comments*. (See section 6.4.) These comments are ignored by the PostScript interpreter, but may be parsed by other software to determine the program's structure:

listing 6-1 ────────────────────────

```
%!PS-Adobe-2.0
%%Title: example
%%Pages: 1
%%BeginProcSet: TextProcs 1.0 0
/F {
      findfont exch scalefont setfont
} bind def
%%EndProcSet
%%EndProlog
%%Page: one 1
 12 /Optima-Oblique F
 100 100 moveto
 (Fairly Oblique) show
 showpage
%%Trailer
```

These structure comments may be used, for example, as guidelines to reverse the pages or to print only one page of many. The last section in this chapter is devoted to these structure comment conventions, but their use here points out the implicit prologue/script structure in the original example program. Adding the comments identifies the program as a *conforming* PostScript language program. These comments should not be included unless the file adheres carefully to the prologue and script model and conforms to the *PostScript Document Structuring Conventions*. The version number to which it conforms is included in the very first line as part of the %!PS-Adobe- comment; in this case, the version is 2.0.

6.3 MODULARITY AND PAGE STRUCTURE

The PostScript language is context-dependent. This means that execution usually depends on previously defined context. The nature of the execution model can be reduced to the following operations, which are typically performed in sequence:

- *Set (or add to)* the state of the interpreter. This could consist of setting the current font, adding to the current path, or making a dictionary entry.

- *Execute* a graphic operation. This includes, for instance, using **show** to print characters, applying **fill** to the current path, or executing **showpage** to print the current page.

Note that the execution of PostScript operators depends to a large extent on the current state of the interpreter (in particular, the graphics state). This is an extremely powerful mechanism, but one which must be understood and used carefully. It is not necessary to program defensively, but it is usually good to isolate the interdependency between page elements as much as possible.

Modularity is an important aspect of program design. It means isolating pieces of code and making them perform independently, with a rigorously defined interface between them. In the PostScript language, this might seem to be hard to accomplish, given the strong dependency upon context. However, by carefully looking at the ground state of the interpreter, the context-dependency can be used to advantage.

GROUND STATE

The *ground state* in a PostScript interpreter is the default context in which all jobs are executed. The ground state of the interpreter is guaranteed to have the following properties:

- The coordinate system (user space) is set up with printer's points as the default measure (72 points to a linear inch), with the origin of the coordinate system placed in the lower left hand of the current page.

- There are no marks on the current page (it need not be erased).

- There is no current path. (This means that there is no current point, either.)

- There is no current font.

- The dictionary stack contains **userdict** and **systemdict** (**userdict** is on the top of the stack).

- All elements of the graphics state have some default setting (for example, butted line end caps, mitered line joins, and black as the current color). The default graphics state is enumerated fully in the *PostScript Language Reference Manual*.

- The current transformation matrix is in its default state (it is machine-dependent).

This context is the starting place for all programs executing on the PostScript interpreter. In order to cooperate effectively with the execution environment, the ground state should be taken to be inviolable. That is, since the page is blank, it should not be erased. Since the graphic state is in its default state, one should not execute **initgraphics**. Only those elements of the interpreter's state which need to *differ* from the ground state should explicitly be set. There are several reasons for this: the programs are simpler; there is usually nothing accomplished by unnecessarily setting default states; if the state of the machine differs from the documented default, it is probably done deliberately. For example, to print pages 2-up requires modification to the current transformation matrix, which **initgraphics** would reset.

Some parts of the graphics state are restored naturally to their default state, and **gsave** and **grestore** may not be necessary. For example, the current point is destroyed naturally by the path painting operators. If a procedure constructs a path and paints it without modifying any other aspects of the ground state, then it need not use **gsave** and **grestore**.

Modularity is best achieved by carefully redefining the ground state and returning to it between elements (modules). That way, every page element, every document page, and every procedure can expect the same initial state. It may be convenient in many cases to use the default state of the PostScript interpreter as the ground state for an application, although a slightly different state can be defined at the beginning of the document and reestablished with **save** and **restore**.

THE OPERAND STACK

The PostScript language provides a uniform, rigorously defined interface between all modules of a program, and it is best to use this system to provide functional independence among modules. This mechanism is simply the operand stack. All parameters are passed via the operand stack, and all operators have very carefully defined semantics in terms of what they expect on the stack and what they will return on the stack. This is inherently the way programmers write PostScript procedures and functions, too, but it is important to realize that it is a definition of the interface between program modules, in addition to being the only reasonable way to pass information.

Use of the operand stack as both an interface and a data structure is covered in Section 2.3. For purposes of examining program modularity, it is enough to think of it as the communications medium between modules of a program.

FUNCTIONAL AND GRAPHIC INDEPENDENCE

Two kinds of failures can result when program modules are not sufficiently independent. They are actually quite different, and must be considered individually:

- Incorrect functional context (execution errors)

- Incorrect graphic interdependency (an unintended picture)

Most programmers are familiar with the first of these: if you don't define a module correctly or pass it the proper parameters, the program fails. the interpreter will usually alert the programmer to this kind of difficulty by executing the **typecheck** or **stackunderflow** errors, for example, although occasionally the program will continue to execute, even though the operands on the stack may not be the right ones.

The second kind of failure mode above, which has been termed "Incorrect graphic interdependency," is typically a conceptual error on the part of the programmer, and can be paraphrased: "It printed, but it did not print as I intended." This is usually the result of a kind of *ripple effect* that occurs when some aspects of the graphics state carry over from one graphic element to another. For example, if the caption under a drawing is linked to the current point after the drawing is executed, the caption may end up in the wrong place if the drawing is changed. Similarly, if the current font at the end of one paragraph is **bold** and it is not explicitly re-set to the "roman" face at the beginning of the next paragraph, the following text may incorrectly print in the **bold** font. Unfortunately, many programs which are poorly designed only get worse as "bugs" like this get fixed. The resulting program, after debugging, is typically *much* more complex than it should be, and is often characterized by unnecessary calls to **gsave** and **grestore** or explicitly executing **0 setgray** at the beginning of every procedure. These kinds of problems usually can be traced to a single procedure that failed to restore the state correctly when it finished executing.

This second kind of *graphic modularity* is perhaps the more important one in terms of designing a driver for an application. Because the order of evaluation for page elements is not enforced when building a page in the PostScript language, it is the programmer's responsibility to determine how (and in what order) to execute the various graphic elements on a page. This typically depends upon the composition software's imaging model, but it must be carefully considered in order to write a modular PostScript language program.

SAVE AND RESTORE

Perhaps the best way to ensure independence between graphic modules is by using the **save** and **restore** mechanism provided in the PostScript language. The **save** and **restore** operators capture a particular state of the interpreter and restore it exactly as it was. In particular, a well-defined ground state may be saved and reclaimed between each graphic element on a page. Each individual component is then free to modify the graphics state in any way which seems appropriate (including scaling, rotating, changing fonts, and so forth), but these changes are guaranteed to be isolated from other page elements by the **save/restore** mechanism.

Since **save** and **restore** are somewhat more expensive than **gsave** and **grestore**, they should only be used where the contents of VM need to be restored as well as the graphics state. They are appropriate at a fairly coarse level, either at each page boundary, or between page elements that consume memory (like text blocks, since the strings require storage space).

There is further information on **save** and **restore** in Section 13.3 and in Section 3.10.

PAGE ELEMENTS AND THEIR PROPERTIES

When designing programs in the PostScript language, characteristic graphic elements should be isolated, each of which may have a set of *properties* associated with it. These properties should be defined to be the set of characteristics that may differ from the ground state. For instance, a line-drawing primitive will have the line weight defined to be one of its properties, since it is useful to be able to provide different line thicknesses. On the other hand, a line-drawing routine need not modify the current font in order to perform correctly. This approach is a formalization of the principle of functional independence. By carefully isolating which aspects of the interpreter's state needs to be changed for each graphic procedure, and by making sure the state is returned afterward, the necessary independence can be achieved simply and effectively.

With this approach, each page element will likely have a particular position on the page as one of its properties. This corresponds to establishing a current point in the graphics state before the code is executed. In many instances, it seems as though the position of a page element depends (or should depend) on some other page element. Part of the work in designing a driver for an application involves determining the interdependency between page elements, both graphically and programmatically.

Listing 6-2 is an example of two routines that have some graphic interdependency. One is called **circle**, the other **square**. Each of them calls the **fill** operator, which makes it implicitly dependent upon the current color. In the example, it can be seen that setting the gray value affects all subsequently drawn circles or squares.

listing 6-2 ───────────────────────────

```
%!PS-Adobe-2.0
%%Title: graphic independence
%%EndComments
/circle { %def
      0 360 arc fill
} bind def
/square { %def
      moveto
      1 index 0 rlineto
      0 exch rlineto
      neg 0 rlineto
      closepath fill
} bind def
%%EndProlog
0.5 setgray
72 100 200 circle
200 300 100 100 square
0 setgray
200 300 300 300 square
showpage
%%Trailer
```

Listing 6-3 shows the same two procedures, slightly rewritten to have the color (gray value) of each shape passed as one of its arguments. This effectively removes the interdependency between the objects. If the shapes are likely to be painted with various gray levels, it is appropriate to pass the shade of gray as one of the attributes for those page elements. This also ensures that the ground state is preserved between page elements, and other procedures can rely on the current color to be as originally defined.

For each graphic element on a page, for each module of the PostScript language driver, you must decide exactly how the elements will behave with respect to one another. A ground state can be defined that is appropriate for all the various elements on a page, and each element can provide any alternate properties that are appropriate.

listing 6-3 ————————————————————————————————

```
%!PS-Adobe-2.0
%%Title: graphic dependence
%%EndComments
/circle { %def
    gsave
        arc setgray fill
    grestore
} bind def
/square { %def
    gsave
        moveto
        1 index 0 rlineto
        0 exch rlineto
        neg 0 rlineto
        closepath setgray fill
    grestore
} bind def
%%EndProlog
0.5   72 100 200 0 360 circle
0.5   200 300 100 100 square
0     200 300 300 300 square
showpage
%%Trailer
```

6.4 DOCUMENT STRUCTURING CONVENTIONS

The *PostScript Document Structuring Conventions* are a formal set of guidelines for PostScript language programs. Program files that observe the guidelines are known as *conforming* files. The purpose of having conforming file standards is to facilitate document interchange and promote the development of print spoolers and font servers. Many documents are composed on a workstation and printed later on one of perhaps several different printing devices. Being able to identify the structure of the file permits greater flexibility to adapt the needs of the document to a particular printer.

The structuring conventions have a tangible representation in the form of PostScript language comments that are embedded in the program file, which delineate its structure. These comments are intended to be parsed and understood by software, rather than humans. The format of the comments should be strictly followed for this reason. It is also understood that a file which claims to be a conforming file (by having the appropriate comments embedded) should indeed conform to the structuring conventions.

The PostScript document structuring conventions are fully documented in a separate document available from Adobe Systems entitled *PostScript Document Structuring Conventions*. They can also be seen in context in most of the program listings in this book, although their use here is minimal, to keep the listings from being lengthy and hard to read. The purpose of the comments is to convey information about the program to parsing software that may be interested in determining its structure (or its resource requirements, such as downloadable fonts). The structuring rules, including page modularity, are required for parallel processing, page reversal, and other document handling needs. Please refer to Chapter 10 for further information on PostScript file interchange standards.

chapter 7

THE MECHANICS OF SETTING TEXT

You shall see them on a beautiful quarto page,
where a neat rivulet of text shall meander
through a meadow of margin.

– Richard Brinsley Sheridan

7.1   INTRODUCTION

Setting text is one of the most common operations performed by many printing applications, and one of the most difficult. There are many aspects of typography and graphic design that can be difficult to accommodate in a computer program. For example, a typesetter may expect justified text, even when it contains different fonts or point sizes, kerning of the text based both on the point size and on specific pairs of letters, and all at the full rated speed of the printer. Setting non-Roman text or using font characters as symbols presents another class of problems but uses the same mechanisms in the PostScript language.

Many of the requirements of setting text are in fact document formatting issues. For instance, establishing margins, laying out lines, or choosing a text point size are decisions that are typically made by a word processing application or some other layout software. Writing a PostScript language driver is the task of converting the document formatter's representation of text into a printable form.

This chapter is devoted to the mechanics of setting text in the PostScript language. A primary focus is efficiency: how to get the job done as fast as possible. Most of the topics are specific to proportional fonts and traditional typography, although the concepts should apply as well to monospaced fonts and special requirements.

Unfortunately, optimizing the text-setting portion of a driver depends to some extent on the nature of the text being set. It may be that an algorithm that works well for setting many lines of text in the same font becomes too slow when fonts are changed frequently, or that a method that assumes line spacing is uniform may be difficult to adapt to display typography. Several different approaches and algorithms are presented in this chapter, and the software designer must choose which ones are appropriate for a particular task. In many instances, it is best to build in several mechanisms, and to invoke one or the other of them depending on the text being set.

Note:

> *There is one principle to keep in mind when deciding upon an algorithm for setting text. The longer the string presented to one of the **show** operators, the more efficient the system is likely to be. This is because the PostScript language built-in operators, such as **show**, **widthshow**, and **ashow**, operate essentially at compiled speed once they have been invoked. Each **moveto** or **div** operation performed must first be interpreted, which is significantly slower.*

7.2 CHARACTER WIDTHS

Formatting text requires access to character width information. In order to decide where to break a line of text, one needs to be able to compute the length of the line of text by adding up the widths of the individual characters in the line. In order to center a heading on a page, one needs to know what the width of the heading is.

Line breaks and centering are formatting issues. Making a decision to break a line is a document-wide decision, since it can affect page breaks or paragraphs, which in turn can affect the rest of the document. Under most circumstances, the formatting of a document is left to document composition systems, and is not appropriate at the printing stage.

The standard approach to document formatting is to make *character metric* information available in a format that can be used by host composition software. All a word processor needs to be able to use a new font is a table with the widths of all the characters in the font. In a screen display system, a set of *screen fonts* may be required, as well, although the pixel widths of the screen characters may or may not be accurate enough for careful typesetting. Usually both width tables and screen fonts are required. Adobe Systems typefaces are made available with separate *metrics files* in a file format designed to be parsed by application software. These files are known as AFM files (for Adobe Font Metrics). A complete description of the format of these files is found in a separate document available from Adobe Systems, entitled *AFM Files: An Interchange Format for POSTSCRIPT® Font Metrics*. These files also contain detailed kerning and ligature information. (Their use is discussed in Section 7.6.)

The *width* of a character is defined to be the amount by which the current point is modified after printing the character. For Roman character sets, the width typically includes the *left* and *right sidebearings*, which are a comfortable amount of space on each side of the character for good letter spacing.

Figure 7.1 is an illustration of four characters (including a space character) from the font StoneSerif (which is also the font you are reading), that shows the character widths and sidebearings.

figure 7.1

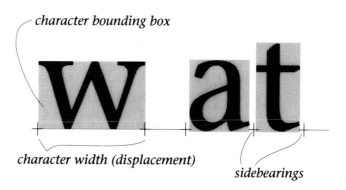

character bounding box

character width (displacement)

sidebearings

Notice that the physical width of the two characters is not quite the same as the optical width of the characters, due to the sidebearings. This is often ignored in ordinary typography, although it can be handled by obtaining the *bounding box* of the characters at each end of the string to determine what the side-bearings are. The bounding box provides the corners of an imaginary rectangle that just touches all the extremes of the character shape (hence "bounding"). This information is given as an offset from the character origin, and therefore provides the left side-bearing directly, and can be subtracted from the width of the character to determine the right side-bearing. The bounding box of each character is also provided in the AFM files.

7.3   MARGINS AND JUSTIFICATION

In setting columns of text (or "body copy") there are often *margins* observed on each side of the lines of text. These margins are usually specified as the amount of white space between the text and the edges of the paper, but this is not a very specific measurement when a document may be printed on more than one size of paper. A better measure probably is to specify the starting point of the text, and the line length of the text. These starting point for the text is certainly needed for setting with the PostScript language. There are four basic types of line layout that are in common use: centered, flush left, flush right, and justified. These are also sometimes referred to as centered, left-justified, right-justified, and fully-justified. In *Figure 7.2* is an example with four text blocks, each of which is set in one of these styles.

One might also want to indent the first line of a paragraph of text or provide unusual borders around which to "flow" text. These can all be handled relatively easily if both the starting point of the text and the particular line length are maintained by the composing application.

figure 7.2

an excerpt from
The Raven
by Edgar Allan Poe
February, 1845

Then this ebony bird beguiling my sad fancy into smiling,
By the grave and stern decorum of the countenance it wore,
"Though thy crest be shorn and shaven, thou," I said, "art sure no craven,
Ghastly grim and ancient Raven wandering from the Nightly shore—
Tell me what thy lordly name is on the Night's Plutonian shore!"
Quoth the Raven "Nevermore."

Much I marvelled this ungainly fowl to hear discourse so plainly, Though its answer little meaning—little relevancy bore; For we cannot help agreeing that no sublunary being Ever yet was blessed with seeing bird above his chamber door—Bird or beast upon the sculptured bust above his chamber door, With such name as "Nevermore."

But the Raven, sitting lonely on the placid bust, spoke only, That one word, as if his soul in that one word he did outpour. Nothing farther then he uttered–not a feather then he fluttered–Till I scarcely more than muttered "Other friends have flown before—On the morrow he will leave me, as my Hopes have flown before." Quoth the Raven "Nevermore."

In *listing 7-1* some procedures are defined that implement "rightshow" and "centershow". These procedures do a fair amount of calculation, and are only appropriate if the widths of the strings cannot be determined at the host (for instance, they might be used in a printer emulator). Generally, the host application will already have determined precisely where the text should be placed, and can simply use **moveto** and **show** for all of the above styles.

These procedures combine the **moveto** and **show** operations. Both the x, y values of the location on the page and the string to be printed are passed on the operand stack. This is faster than doing separate name lookup and execution on both **moveto** and **show**. Notice that the margins are maintained by the host application, and an explicit location on the page is passed for each string.

listing 7-1 ———————————————————

```
%!PS-Adobe-2.0
%%Title: margin procedures
%%BeginProcSet: text-procs 1.0 0
% moveto-show
/SH { %def
    moveto show
} bind def
% rightshow
/RS { %def
    moveto
    dup stringwidth neg exch neg exch
    rmoveto show
} bind def
%centershow
/CS { %def
    moveto dup stringwidth
    2 div neg exch 2 div neg exch
    rmoveto show
} bind def
%%EndProcSet: text-procs 1.0 0
%%EndProlog
/Times-Roman findfont 14 scalefont setfont
(Centered about + current point) 306 140 CS
(+Flush Left at current point) 72 120 SH
(Flush Right at current point+) 560 120 RS
showpage
%%Trailer
```

JUSTIFICATION

For standard text-setting, the natural letter spacing and word spacing should be used. Letters may be kerned to improve their visual spacing (see section 7.6), but the lines of text should usually not be stretched in any way unless it is necessary to justify the text.

There are two levels of refinement for justifying a column of text:

- Provide careful hyphenation and word breaking to get the lines of text as close as possible to the correct length.

- Modify the word spacing as necessary to stretch the text to fit the necessary width of the line.

Under normal circumstances, the inter-letter spacing *should not be modified at all*. The legibility of text tends to suffer greatly when letter spacing is compromised. If hyphenation is not available, or when it cannot be avoided, both word and letter spacing can be modified simultaneously with the **awidthshow** operator.

The appropriate way to modify word spacing is to use the **widthshow** operator, which was designed with this purpose in mind. **widthshow** prints text just as **show** does, except that it modifies the character width of a particular character by the specified amount while it is printing it. By supplying a small amount by which to change the width of the space character, word spacing can be modified quite efficiently and easily. *Listing 7-2* contains an example of its use.

listing 7-2 —————————————————————————

```
%!PS-Adobe-2.0
%%Title: widthshow example
/F {
        findfont exch scalefont setfont
} bind def
/W /widthshow load def
%%EndProlog
%%BeginSetup
/sp 32 def  % ASCII space
%%EndSetup
36 745 moveto
24 /Times-Italic F
6 0 sp (PostScript Language Program Design) W
showpage
%%Trailer
```

The computation that needs to be performed is to determine the amount by which to modify the width of the space character. For justified text, the space modifier (**SpaceMod**) is the intended line width (**LineWidth**) less the width of the existing string (**StringWidth**) divided by the number of spaces in the string (**Spaces**). This computation can easily be performed by the host application if the character widths are known.

$$\textbf{SpaceMod} = \frac{(\textbf{LineWidth - StringWidth})}{\textbf{Spaces}}$$

This **SpaceMod** quantity is passed directly to the **widthshow** operator each time it is called. Notice that this value will be different for every line of text, since there are likely to be different numbers of spaces (and different string widths) for each line.

7.4 HANDLING DIFFERENT FONTS

Justifying lines of text in which there may be font changes (or point size changes) requiring several instances of **show** require more careful computation to determine the exact position of each of the components.

The larger the string that is provided to **show**, the more efficient the driver will be. It is best to break each line into as few pieces as necessary to accomplish the task. For instance, using **widthshow** to modify word spacing is superior to using repetitive **moveto** and **show** operations.

Listing 7-3 contains an approach for setting a single line of text with multiple font changes. The method used is to **show** all parts of the line that are in the same font at the same time. This means first finding, say, all the roman parts of the string and showing them (put each substring on the stack with its individual *x* position). Then showing all the bold parts (they could as well be a completely different font), and so on. This is a somewhat unusual approach, and requires some careful setup work on the host system, but it will likely be quite fast when there are many font changes. It also provides a natural framework for handling downloadable fonts, since the text is grouped by font used, not by context on a line. *Figure 7.3* shows the output of this program.

listing 7-3 ─────────────────────────────────

```
%!PS-Adobe-2.0
%%Title: mixed-font text setting
/FS { %def
      findfont exch scalefont
} bind def
/SF { %def
      Fonts exch get setfont
} bind def
/MS {   %multiple "show"
      counttomark 2 idiv { %repeat
          0 moveto show
      } repeat pop
      mark
} bind def
/LINE { %def
      gsave
      translate
      mark                    % mark is for MS procedure
} bind def
/S { %def
      moveto show
} bind def
/END { %def
      pop grestore
} bind def
%%EndProlog
%%BeginSetup
/Fonts [ %def
          12 /Times-Roman FS
          12 /Times-Bold FS
          12 /Times-Italic FS
] def
%%EndSetup
%%BeginObject: text_block
0 SF
save                    % text block ground state
% first line of text
72 312 LINE          % first line start
(Here is a line with ) 0
```

```
(words and ) 140.315
(words.) 238.991
MS
2 SF
(two ) 192.971
(italic ) 112.644
MS
1 SF
(bold ) 213.311
(two ) 90.984
MS
END
% lines 2, 3, and 4 in the text:
(You shall see them on a beautiful quarto) 72 288 S
(page, where a neat rivulet of text shall) 72 276 S
(meander through a meadow of margin.) 72 264 S
% credit for quotation:
160 240 LINE
 2 SF
 (Richard Brinsley Sheridan) 0
 MS
END
restore                    % to ground state
%%EndObject
showpage
%%Trailer
```

---

figure 7.3

Here is a line with **two** *italic* words and *two* **bold** words.

You shall see them on a beautiful quarto
page, where a neat rivulet of text shall
meander through a meadow of margin.

Richard Brinsley Sheridan

7.5 LEADING AND POINT SIZE

Leading is the distance between lines of text. In the days of metal (lead) type, it referred to actual strips of lead placed between two rows of type to increase the spacing between them. In contemporary computer typesetting, the value typically refers to the *baseline-to-baseline* distance between two lines of text, rather than the distance from the bottom of one line to the top of the next. Within the context of this book, leading refers to the distance between baselines.

There are practically no rules governing the height of individual letterforms in digital fonts. The *point size* of a font is the metric by which the font is chosen and set. Originally, the point size of a lead font was a measure of the slug in which the letterform was cast. Today, digital outline fonts are not restricted at all in terms of point size, and the size does not necessarily reflect the height of the characters, the bounding box, or anything else. Although information is typically provided for the *capital height*, the *x-height*, and perhaps the *ascender* and *descender* heights, these metrics are not guaranteed to be consistent even across any individual font, and especially not from one font to another. In general, no assumptions should be made about the relationship between the actual height of characters a font and the point size. (See *figure 7.4*.)

figure 7.4

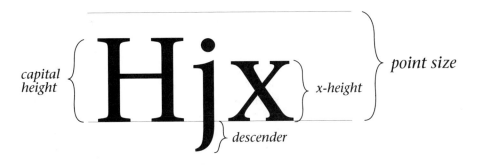

7.6 KERNING AND LIGATURES

Kerning is a modification to inter-letter spacing of text. Kerning is applied with proportionally spaced typefaces for purely visual reasons: either because it looks better, or because it improves the legibility of the text.

There are two varieties of kerning: *pairwise* kerning and *track* kerning. Pairwise kerning is an adjustment to the inter-letter spacing between a particular pair of letters. There is usually a table of values stored for each font. Since the motivation for kerning is purely visual, there is no easy way to do it algorithmically. Track kerning is a change to the inter-letter spacing of an entire line of text, based on the point size of the font used. For instance, smaller type should be set slightly wider than normal, and very large type (*display type*) should be spaced closer together. Again, the reasons are optical. (See *figure 7.5*.)

figure 7.5

Kerning, at its simplest, involves an adjustment of the current point after the first character of a pair. This is effectively the same as temporarily changing the character width, depending on the following character. The second character is set normally, although it may itself be a candidate for beginning another kern pair. The **rmoveto** operator is suited to adjusting the current point, as in the following example. However, it should be worked carefully into whatever text-setting algorithm is used.

```
%!PS-Adobe-2.0
%%EndComments
/S /show load def
/r /rmoveto load def
%%EndProlog
/StoneSerif findfont 48 scalefont setfont
100 100 moveto
(A) S -5.5 0 r
(W) S -6.8 0 r
(A) S -5 0 r
(Y) S
showpage
```

There is a bit of unnecessary interpreter overhead for each character printed, in this example. This can be tightened up a bit, using the **kshow** operator; notice that the values for **rmoveto** are based on the user-space coordinate system. If the text were set at a different point size, these values would be different, as in the following example:

```
%!PS-Adobe-2.0
%%EndComments
/K { %def
        { pop pop 0 rmoveto } exch kshow
} bind def
%%EndProlog
/StoneSerif findfont 48 scalefont setfont
100 100 moveto
-5 -6.8 -5.5 (AWAY) K
showpage
```

This procedure minimizes some of the interpreter overhead, since fewer name lookups are performed, and since **bind** is performed on the procedure body. The main drawback of this approach is that **kshow** will always execute the procedure between every pair of characters in the string. If no kerning is desired, **0** must still be supplied on the stack (resulting in the unnecessary execution of **0 0 rmoveto**). The viability of this approach depends on the amount of kerning that needs to be done. If only an occasional pair of characters is kerned, this is not a good approach. However, if every letter is positioned individually, the **K** procedure above might be a good choice.

Another approach to kerning is to use a negative width space character, and actually put the character in between the pair of letters to be kerned. The **show** operator will then automatically adjust the position based on the width of the kern character. The only difficulty with this is that in order to provide enough flexibility in kern values, many space characters of varying widths are required. It is also more difficult for the composing application to insert the extra space characters wherever kerning is required.

Listing 7-4 contains a good hybrid approach. A line of text is set by breaking it into pieces that are as long as possible, and placing all the strings on the operand stack along with some extra information. There are three variations on the theme: **stackshow**, which prints several strings on the stack, each with a different font (supplied on the stack); **kernstackshow**, which performs the same operation but permits a value for **rmoveto** between strings; **kernshow**, which permits kerning values but not font changes. Each of them provides for a fast approach to setting text, where the component strings are made as long as possible, depending on the lines of text in the host application.

listing 7-4 ─────────────────────────────────────

```
%!PS-Adobe-2.0
%%Title: text-procs.ps
%%Creator: Glenn Reid, Adobe Systems
%%EndComments
%%BeginProcSet: general 1.0 0
/F { findfont exch scalefont setfont } bind def
/Fdef { findfont exch scalefont def } bind def
/M /moveto load def
%%EndProcSet: general 1.0 0

%%BeginProcSet: text-procs 1.0 0
% mark (text) fontdict (text) fontdict ... stackshow
/stackshow { %def
    % reverse stack order first:
        2 2 counttomark 2 sub { -2 roll } for
        counttomark 2 idiv { %repeat
            setfont show
        } repeat pop
} bind def
```

chapter 7 THE MECHANICS OF SETTING TEXT

```
% mark (Txt) font rX rY ... kernstackshow
/kernstackshow { %def
        4 4 counttomark 2 sub { -4 roll } for
        counttomark 4 idiv { %repeat
            rmoveto setfont show
        } repeat pop
} bind def
```

```
% "kernshow" is like "stackshow" except that it does
% not use a font dictionary for each string.  It
% should be used when the kerned text is all set in
% the same font.
```

```
% mark (text) rX rY (text) rX rY .... kernshow
/kernshow { %def
        3 3 counttomark 2 sub { -3 roll } for
        counttomark 3 idiv { %repeat
            rmoveto show
        } repeat pop
} bind def
```

```
/MM { moveto mark } bind def
%%EndProcSet: text-procs 1.0 0
%%EndProlog
%%BeginSetup
/F1 50 /StoneSerif Fdef
/F2 50 /StoneSerif-Semibold Fdef
/F3 50 /StoneSerif-Italic Fdef
%%EndSetup
%%Page: 1 1
F1 setfont
36 430 MM
    (S) 0 0 (W) -4 0 (EPT A)
    -4 0 (W) -8.0 0 (A) -9.25 0 (Y) -6.75 0
kernshow
36 380 MM
    (S) F1 0 0 (W) F1 -4 0 (EPT ) F1 -4 0
    (A) F3 -4 0 (W) F3 -8.0 0
    (A) F3 -9.25 0 (Y) F3 -6.75 0
kernstackshow

showpage
%%Trailer
```

Ligatures are also used to improve the visual quality of text. These are specially designed characters that comprise two (or even three) sequential letterforms. For instance, the two letters *f* and *i*, when set together, may be combined into a single shape: *fi*. This can affect composition software since the width of the fi ligature is usually different than the sum of the widths of the *f* and *i* characters. (See *figure 7.6*; the font is Stone Serif-Italic.) Ligatures cannot usually be added to a font—they are part of the original font design. However, the application should recognize and replace sequential instances of, say, *f* and *i*, with the single *fi* ligature character. Spelling checkers, hyphenation tables, and justification algorithms need to know about them, as well.

figure 7.6

Use of the fi ligature

7.7 ENCODING AND CHARACTER SETS

A typical PostScript language font program is a collection of procedures, each with a particular name, stored into a dictionary. Each of these procedures, when executed, draws one character shape. There are other entries in a font dictionary, but all of them are used to set up or execute one of the character-drawing procedures.

The collection of character procedures that are stored in a font is known as the *character set* of that font. There can be any number of these character procedures stored in the font dictionary. There is no limitation (other than available memory) on the total number of characters. There is, however, a limitation on how many of them can be accessed at any particular moment.

Access to font characters is controlled through the encoding mechanism.

The characters in a font currently must be accessed by *character code*. A string presented to the **show** operator can be thought of simply as a sequence of ASCII bytes, each of which is actually just an index into the encoding vector for the current font. The *encoding vector* is an array of 256 name objects, each of which should be the name of a procedure stored in the font dictionary. The **show** operator actually presents the integer character code to the **BuildChar** procedure in each font, and it is up to that procedure to invoke the correct character description.

This mechanism was deliberately set up to provide an easy way to change the mapping between the codes in the string and the characters that are actually selected from the font. Each font dictionary is required (by **definefont**) to have an array named **/Encoding** as one of its top-level entries. To reencode a font, copy the font dictionary, put in a different **Encoding** vector, and rename the font. *Listing 7-5* contains a good reencoding algorithm. It is designed to avoid having to provide redundant data. A block of sequentially encoded names can be specified by providing only the initial encoding value—the others are assigned in sequence.

listing 7-5 ———————————————————————————————

```
%!PS-Adobe-2.0
%%Title: reencode.ps
%%EndComments
/F { %def
     findfont exch scalefont setfont
} bind def
%%BeginProcSet: reencode 1.0 0
% This file defines a procedure called "R" which
% reencodes a font.  It expects three objects on the
% stack:
%
%    [array] /NewName /OldName
%
% The array should contain pairs of
%    <number> <name>,
% like "32 /space", each of which defines a slot in the
% encoding and the name to put in that slot.  Only
```

```
% those names that are needed to over-ride the
% existing ones should be specified.  An encoding
% value (number) may be specified followed by more
% than one name, like  "128 /name1 /name2".
% In this case, the names will be sequentially stored
% in the encoding starting at the initial number
% given (128).
 /RE { %def
     findfont begin
     currentdict dup length dict begin
         { %forall
             1 index /FID ne {def} {pop pop} ifelse
         } forall
         /FontName exch def dup length 0 ne { %if
             /Encoding Encoding 256 array copy def
             0 exch { %forall
                 dup type /nametype eq { %ifelse
                     Encoding 2 index 2 index put
                     pop 1 add
                 }{ %else
                     exch pop
                 } ifelse
             } forall
         } if pop
     currentdict dup end end
     /FontName get exch definefont pop
 } bind def
%%EndProcSet: reencode 1.0 0
%%EndProlog
%%BeginSetup
/stdencoding [ 39/quotesingle 96/grave
  128/Adieresis/Aring/Ccedilla/Eacute/Ntilde
  /Odieresis/Udieresis/aacute/agrave/acircumflex
  /adieresis/atilde/aring/ccedilla/eacute/egrave/ecircumflex
  /edieresis/iacute/igrave/icircumflex/idieresis/ntilde/oacute
  /ograve/ocircumflex/odieresis/otilde/uacute/ugrave
  /ucircumflex/udieresis/dagger/.notdef/cent/sterling/section
  /bullet/paragraph/germandbls/registered/copyright
  /trademark/acute/dieresis/.notdef/AE/Oslash/.notdef
  /.notdef/.notdef/.notdef/yen/.notdef/.notdef/.notdef/.notdef
  /.notdef/.notdef/ordfeminine/ordmasculine/.notdef/ae/oslash
  /questiondown/exclamdown/logicalnot/.notdef/florin
  /.notdef/.notdef/guillemotleft/guillemotright/ellipsis/.notdef
  /Agrave/Atilde/Otilde/OE/oe/endash/emdash/quotedblleft
  /quotedblright/quoteleft/quoteright/.notdef/.notdef
  /ydieresis/Ydieresis/fraction/currency/guilsinglleft
  /guilsinglright/fi/fl/daggerdbl/periodcentered
  /quotesinglbase/quotedblbase/perthousand/Acircumflex
  /Ecircumflex/Aacute/Edieresis/Egrave/Iacute/Icircumflex
  /Idieresis/Igrave/Oacute/Ocircumflex/.notdef/Ograve
  /Uacute/Ucircumflex/Ugrave/dotlessi/circumflex/tilde
```

```
/macron/breve/dotaccent/ring/cedilla/hungarumlaut
/ogonek/caron
] def
stdencoding /_StoneSerif /StoneSerif RE
stdencoding /_StoneSerif-Italic /StoneSerif-Italic RE
%%EndSetup
90 /_StoneSerif-Italic F
50 220 moveto (fig. \336ve) show
showpage
%%Trailer
```

7.8   COMPOSITE CHARACTERS AND ACCENTS

Many languages require accented characters that may not be
included in the standard character set. Most of the necessary
characters can be derived from combining existing glyphs in the
font. These are known as *composite* characters. Some composite
characters are already included in fonts from Adobe Systems, but
are not encoded. (They are not present in the **StandardEncoding** vector that is used in most fonts.) These can be accessed by
merely reencoding the font. (See the previous example program). However, for character combinations which are not
already included in the font, some extra steps must be taken to
set up the fonts.

7.9   NON-ROMAN FONTS

Many of the assumptions that are made about setting text can
be challenged by a font that does not contain a standard Roman
alphabet as its character set. In particular, a font may in fact be a
collection of *graphic objects*, each of which can call upon the
entire richness of the PostScript language during its execution.
Notions of point size, leading, and kerning can take on a different meaning when fonts are used for such purposes. In many
ways, display typography requires placement of letterforms as
graphic objects, and some of the generalized rules for placement given in this section apply directly to display type.

CHARACTER WIDTHS AND ORIGINS

The correct way to think about a character in a PostScript font is that it is anchored at the *character origin*, and that the current point is displaced by the character width vector after the glyph has been drawn. Remember that character widths in PostScript fonts have both an *x* and a *y* component. The current point may be modified as appropriate for specific character sequences.

For example, let us look at a few characters from a music notation font, *Sonata*. There are characters in the font which are designed much like *accents* are designed in other fonts: They are intended to be used as *composite* elements to build up other characters. *Figure 7.7* shows three characters from *Sonata*: the **quarternotehead**, the **upstem**, and the **sxflagup**. Alongside them is the composite character that can be built by painting these characters sequentially. The sixteenth flag character and the upward stem both have a width displacement of **0** in both *x* and *y*. That means that the current point does not move at all after the character has been printed. This permits characters to be superimposed one on top of another. It also provides perfect registration of the shapes, with no possibility of position round-off error. The final notehead character does have a width, and the current point is left just to the right of the notehead character after it is printed. Notice also the offset from the origin that is inherent to the two composite characters. They are designed to register exactly with the character.

figure 7.7

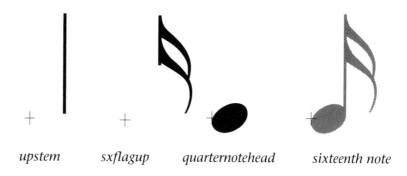

upstem   sxflagup   quarternotehead   sixteenth note

When the three characters are set together, a sixteenth note results. Using one additional character (**extendflagup**) provides the capability of building arbitrarily complicated notes. In this case, the current point is adjusted between characters, but is restricted to vertical movement. The alignment of the characters is guaranteed by their design. (See *figure 7.8.*) Working with text characters which are in fact used more as graphic symbols than as conventional text requires some careful thought. The same design guidelines apply for using **setfont** and **show** with Sonata as they would with StoneSerif. The fewer operations (and the more characters that can be printed at once with a single call to **show**), the better the performance will be.

There are applications for which specialized fonts can be a big advantage. For instance, CAD/CAM applications may build a library of symbols that may be used within a diagram. If they are used as font characters, then the speed of the font cache can dramatically decrease printing time for diagrams with many symbols. The font should be carefully designed so that it can be used with maximum efficiency, and the character widths and origins planned around where the current point should be.

figure 7.8

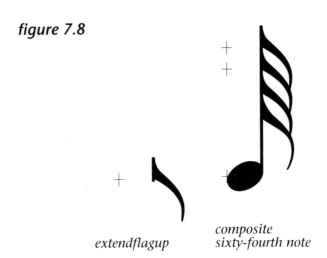

extendflagup

composite
sixty-fourth note

Arranging characters on a page is the realm of word-processing or page composition software. In order to work with non-Latin character sets, many of the built-in assumptions about text must be relaxed. For example, word wrapping, line spacing, and hyphenation are very closely tied to languages which read left to right, which set characters on a common baseline, and which have very little variation in vertical placement of characters. Setting text in Arabic, Kanji, Urdu, Mathematics, or other languages require much more sophisticated placement algorithms and judgement. Working with these languages in the PostScript language can be reduced to two characteristic issues:

• Knowing the *origin* of the characters is crucial to placing it in the correct position.

• The *character width* affects the placement of the following character.

Adjusting the current point slightly after printing a character is called kerning when setting most languages with the Roman alphabet. Kerning is often considered optional and it is a refinement to typesetting. In other languages, the current point may need to be adjusted between every two characters on the page, depending on the context, and it is not considered optional. This is not really a kerning problem, but an issue of placement. But the same principles hold as with all typesetting

chapter 7 THE MECHANICS OF SETTING TEXT

done with the PostScript language—if more than one character can be passed to **show** at once, there will be a significant performance gain over individually placing each character. Some of the burden for this lies on the type designer, and some on the careful placement algorithms used by the layout software.

chapter 8

SCANNED IMAGES AND HALFTONES

"This affair must all be unraveled from within."
He tapped his forehead. "These little gray cells...."

– Agatha Christie

8.1   INTRODUCTION

The **image** operator is the mechanism in the PostScript language for printing sampled images of any size in up to 256 shades of gray. These images may be printed at any size and orientation with a minimum of calculation. The PostScript language also has a built-in digital halftoning system that permits full control of the rendering of gray shades with halftone screens. This chapter takes an in-depth look at the **image** operator and the halftone mechanism.

8.2   THE **IMAGE** OPERATOR

The **image** operator takes data representing an image made up of many small samples and renders it on the current page at a specified location, size, and rotation. The data represents an image that is a certain number of samples wide and high (represented herein by the width and height, respectively). Each sample is represented by a one-, two-, four-, or eight-bit value that assigns a shade of gray to that sample. Each sample will be eventually printed as a black, white, or gray rectangle on the output page. (Color PostScript devices will have additional operators to implement full color images.)

The **image** operator requires five arguments on the operand stack. These are as follows:

- The *width* of the image, in samples. For an 8-bit deep image, this number is the same as the number of bytes in one row of source data.

- The *height* of the image, in samples (or scan lines).

- The number of *bits per sample* in the original data. A black-and-white scanned image has 1 bit per sample, a grayscale image may have 2, 4, or 8 bits per sample.

- The *image matrix*, which is a transformation matrix that maps user space onto the coordinate system implied by the scanning process in the original data.

- The *data acquisition procedure*, which fetches sample data and leaves it on the operand stack as a string object.

HOW IT WORKS

The **image** operator multiplies *width* times *height* times *bits per sample* to determine how many bits of data are needed to render the image. It then executes the *data acquisition procedure* as many times as necessary, imaging each string directly into device space as it is produced by the procedure. The mapping provided by the image matrix is applied as the data is being imaged.

THE IMAGE MATRIX

Sampled data (perhaps from a digitized photograph) has an implicit coordinate system imposed on it by the scanning process. The first sample scanned is, in effect, in position *0,0*. The second sample, assuming a horizontal scan, would be in position *1,0* and so on.

When the **image** operator prints this sampled image in user space, it assigns a particular position in user space to each sample. Thus, there is a coordinate transformation between user space and "sample space" that is involved in the printing of a sampled image.

The image matrix that is passed to the **image** operator is the transformation matrix that provides the transformation between the region in user space the final printed image should occupy and the region in sample space that the image originally occupied.

Since either the user space transformation or the image matrix may be modified independently, there are an infinite number of combinations that will produce the desired image. It is best to hold one of the matrices as a constant entity, and adjust the other one based on the image being rendered.

Here are some steps that will simplify use of the image matrix, and provide a generally correct mapping for any image data into the user coordinate space.

- Use **translate**, **rotate**, and **scale** to alter user space so that a one-unit square at the origin would occupy a space on the current page exactly where you want the image to be printed. That is, if the lower-left corner of the image is to be 3 inches to the right and 10 inches above the current user space origin, and the image is to occupy a space 1 inch wide and 2 inches tall, precede the call to the **image** operator with the lines

    save
    216 720 translate
    72 144 scale

- Invoke the **image** operator, supplying an image matrix that prints the sampled image in the one-unit square at the origin. This matrix is a very easy one to calculate. Images scanned bottom-up and top-down require the following image matrices, respectively:

    [**w 0 0 h 0 0**] *if scanned from the bottom*
    [**w 0 0 -h 0 h**] *if scanned from the top*

    where *w* and *h* are the width and height of the sample data in samples (not points). For a more complete discussion of the image matrix, see Section 4.7 of the *PostScript Language Reference Manual*.

- Provide a data acquisition procedure. This is covered more fully in the next section.

DATA ACQUISITION PROCEDURES

The data acquisition procedure is a PostScript language procedure body used by the **image** operator. It is the responsibility of this procedure to obtain some amount of sampled data, put this data into a string, and leave the string on the operand stack. The **image** operator will call the data acquisition procedure as many times as necessary, each time using the string left on the operand the stack, until it has received an amount of data equal to the (*width x height x bits-per-sample*) as provided to the **image** operator.

The **image** operator processes the data within the string most significant bit first. Thus, the string

(T)

left on the stack would be interpreted by the **image** operator as the string of bits

01010100

This is the binary representation of the decimal number *84,* the ASCII character code of the *T* character.

These bits would be interpreted 1, 2, 4, or 8 at a time to represent the gray value of successive samples (as specified by the *bits-per-sample* value passed to the **image** operator*).*

The data acquisition procedure used in a particular instance depends upon the amount and nature of the data making up the image.

When using strings to represent binary data, careful calculation is necessary to match the amount of data provided to the amount of data that the **image** operator expects to receive. This is especially tricky if 2 or 4 bits per sample are used.

For example, let us suppose an image is 10 samples wide and 8 scan lines high, and each sample consists of 4 bits of grayscale information. The call to **image** will look something like this:

10 8 4 [10 0 0 8 0 0] { datastring } image

The width and height of the image are handed directly to the **image** operator on the operand stack. The **datastring**, however, must be of the appropriate length to match the dimensions of the image. Strings contain 8-bit bytes. To represent **10 x 8 x 4** bits of image data, *320 bits* of information are needed, which requires a *40 byte* string to contain the 320 bits.

SMALL AMOUNTS OF DATA

If the image is made up of a very small amount of data—a few dozen bytes or less—it may be most convenient to let the data acquisition procedure place the string directly on the stack. That is, the procedure may look something like this:

{ <013f8e40ae183d022f> }

The angle brackets in PostScript language syntax denote a *hexadecimal* (base 16) string. Each *pair* of characters represents, in hexadecimal, *eight bits* of information, or a single byte in the string. Thus, the above example would leave a *nine*-character data string on the operand stack, or 72 bits worth of image data.

This form is most appropriate for small images such as printed representations of screen characters or icon bit maps. The *PostScript Language Tutorial and Cookbook* has several examples of this kind of data acquisition procedure.

LARGE AMOUNTS OF DATA

Printing a scanned photograph or other large sampled image requires much more data than can be placed in virtual memory at once. In these cases, the data should be sent to the printer "in line" with the PostScript program, immediately following the call to the **image** operator. The data acquisition procedure must arrange to read the input stream, placing the incoming data into a string in conveniently sized increments.

The following program fragment incorporates such a data acquisition procedure:

```
/DataString 512 string def
512 340 8 [ 512 0 0 -340 0 340 ]
{
```

```
            currentfile DataString readhexstring pop
          } bind image
          f6b94f...
```

This program fragment prints an image consisting of 512 columns of 340 rows each, where each image pixel has a gray scale specified by an 8-bit value. The image matrix indicates that the data represents an image scanned from the top down.

The **readhexstring** operator takes a string object and a file object (in this case the *current file*, which is the file object that is currently being read by the PostScript interpreter). It reads ASCII hexadecimal data from the file and places the data into the string until either the string is full or the end of file has been reached. The **readhexstring** operator returns a string object on the operand stack containing data read from the file, and a boolean object which is **false** if the end of file was reached before the string was filled and **true** otherwise.

In the previous example, the boolean value returned by **read-hexstring** was popped from the stack for efficiency, since the procedure will be called many times by the **image** operator. For debugging purposes, or for better error recovery, it is best to interrogate the resulting boolean and provide some sort of error message if the end-of-file indication was reached prematurely.

The **readhexstring** operator takes the incoming data two characters at a time, interpreting each pair and producing a single byte in the resulting data string. It ignores all characters that are not valid hexadecimal digits, so that the data may include tabs, spaces, newline characters, and so forth.

The ASCII hex representation of the sample data should immediately follow the call to the **image** operator, as in our example above. The data acquisition procedure is called repeatedly, taking characters from the input stream until the entire 512-by-340-by-8-bit image has been processed. At that point, the input stream will be passed back to the PostScript interpreter and the original program can resume.

chapter 8 SCANNED IMAGES AND HALFTONES

A COMMON ERROR AND ITS CAUSE

A common problem when using the **image** operator results from a mismatch between the amount of data supplied and the size of the buffer used by the **readhexstring** operator. In particular, if the *height* times *width* of the image is not evenly divisible by the size of the buffer, **readhexstring** will keep reading the input stream, looking for as much hexadecimal as it can find (remember that it just skips anything that is not valid hexadecimal data). This usually means that the word **showpage** (or any other part of the program) is treated as data, and the **a** and **e** characters from **showpage** are read into the string buffer as hexadecimal values (the others are ignored). If **readhexstring** encounters an end-of-file indication, it returns the boolean **false**. However, as in the example above, this value is ignored (by popping it), and the premature end-of-file condition is not recognized. The symptom of this is that the page simply does not print. Nothing in this scenario provokes an execution error, because each component of the system is behaving as it is supposed to—but the result is not what was intended.

SYNTHETIC DATA

The data handed to the **image** operator can be generated directly by the program. For example, *listing 8-1* supplies a synthetic data string to the **image** operator each time the data acquisition procedure is called; in this case, the string is the same each time and represents a gray-scale "fountain" with 256 possible gray levels (although not all of them will be attainable on low-resolution devices).

This somewhat unusual approach builds a string of 256 bytes, each of which ranges from 0 to 255 sequentially (the **for** loop accomplishes this, although cryptically). When the **image** operator uses this string, each image sample is an 8-bit value, and the values range continuously from 0 to 255 each of these image samples is interpreted as a gray value which is then rendered with the halftone mechanism. The actual number of gray levels achieved in the fountain will depend on the constraints of the current halftone screen frequency and the resolution of the output device, but the transition between them will be as smooth as possible.

listing 8-1 ————————————————

```
%!PS-Adobe-2.0
%%EndComments
/DataString 256 string def
/IM { %def
    gsave translate scale image grestore
} bind def
%%EndProlog
0 1 255 { DataString exch dup put } bind for
1 256 8 [1 0 0 256 0 0] { DataString }
72 72  144 36 IM
showpage
%%Trailer
```

The **translate** and **scale** operations in the **IM** procedure locate the image and stretch it to the desired size. The image is rendered as a single sample in width, with a height of 256 samples. The image matrix provided maps this into the unit square in user space, and the **scale** stretches it to be exactly a 1-inch square on the final page. (See *figure 8.1*.)

figure 8.1

Note that, although this image is 1 sample wide and 256 samples high, the printed size of the image is 1 inch square. Remember that the size of the printed image is determined by the arguments passed to the **scale** operator, not by the number of rows and columns in the sampled data.

8.3 DATA COMPRESSION

Since the **image** operator provides a generalized mechanism for acquiring data (the data acquisition procedure), the data may be compressed on the host system and decompressed by the PostScript interpreter after it has been transmitted to the PostScript device. This may drastically reduce transmission time, but it is quite difficult to make the procedure fast enough to realize a net gain in overall evaluation time.

8.4 HALFTONE SCREENS

Traditional printing methods cannot vary the tone or shade of ink placed on paper. That is, printing technology allows only one shade of ink to be placed on the paper at a time. Multi-color jobs are printed in several passes, one for each color, or they simulate shades of color by halftoning.

Halftoning is familiar to anyone who has looked closely at newspaper photographs. This technique reproduces shades of gray in a final print with small black dots whose sizes are determined by the desired shade of gray. The larger the dots, the darker the gray that the eye will perceive. Another technique is to use very thin lines that grow thicker with increasingly dark gray levels.

Traditionally the way this was accomplished was to lay a halftone screen across the image and photograph the original through the screen. A halftone screen had a certain number of black dots or lines per inch, and were referred to by this number (for instance, a "60 line screen"). This number is reflected in the *frequency* parameter that is provided in the PostScript language halftoning mechanism.

HALFTONING IN THE POSTSCRIPT LANGUAGE

The PostScript language halftone mechanism parallels the traditional methods both in terminology and in technology. The "screen" may be specified at various *frequencies* and *angles*, and the shape of the *spot* can be specified through an executable function.

The PostScript interpreter prints shades of gray with a digital approximation of true halftoning. The dots that a PostScript printer produces are grouped into a square called a *halftone cell*. On a 300 dot-per-inch printer using a 60-line halftone screen and an angle of 0 degrees, this cell is 5 device pixels on a side. Each gray level is rendered by turning more pixels on in the halftone cell, and a gray area is provided by "tiling" the area with these halftone cells.

Most PostScript interpreters by default print black within the halftone cells in such a way that each halftone cell looks like a single dot that expands as the gray gets darker, as in the fountain in *figure 8.1*. This is similar to the results of traditional halftoning; it is known informally as a dot pattern.

CHANGING THE HALFTONE SCREEN

The PostScript language allows you to change the halftone screen by which it represents grays with the **setscreen** operator. This operator takes three arguments:

- *Frequency:* the number of halftone cells per inch.

- *Angle*: the angle from the horizontal by which the halftone cells are rotated.

- *Spot Function:* a procedure body that defines the shape of the halftone spot.

In *listing 8-2* is a short program that changes the frequency of the halftone mechanism to 20 lines per linear inch.

listing 8-2 ⸺⸺⸺⸺⸺⸺⸺⸺⸺⸺⸺⸺⸺⸺⸺⸺⸺⸺⸺⸺

```
%!PS-Adobe-2.0
%%EndComments
/F { findfont exch scalefont setfont } bind def
/setF { %def
    currentscreen
    4 -2 roll pop    % remove existing frequency
    3 1 roll setscreen
} bind def
%%EndProlog
gsave
    20 setF
    .4 setgray
    250 90 moveto
    300 /StoneSerif-Italic F
    (&) show
grestore
showpage
%%Trailer
```

Figure 8.2 shows a gray character rendered with the screen frequency set to **20** as *listing 8-2*. Notice that the other parameters of the halftone machinery are left at their current settings, rather than explicitly setting them. It is best not to disturb them unless you need to replace them. The **setF** procedure replaces only the frequency by using **currentscreen** to get the current screen parameters and **roll** to reposition the arguments on the stack appropriately.

figure 8.2

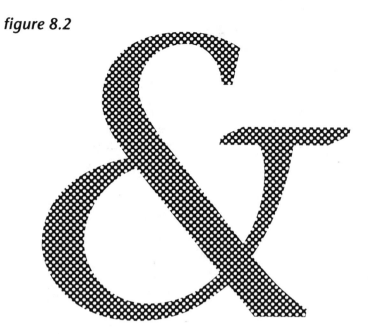

8.5 THE SPOT FUNCTION

The **setscreen** operator considers the halftone cell to be centered on a set of coordinate axes, with the cell extending for one unit in each direction. (See *figure 8.3*.) The spot function supplied to the **setscreen** operator must calculate a priority for each location within the halftone cell.

figure 8.3

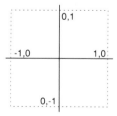

The spot function is handed the *x* and *y* coordinates on the operand stack that represent the location of the center of each device pixel found in the halftone cell. The function must calculate a priority value in the range *-1* to *1* for each position. The halftone mechanism will turn on spots within the halftone cell in order from high to low priority.

For example, the following call to **setscreen** causes the PostScript interpreter to render gray levels with a line screen, instead of a dot screen:

```
%!PS-Adobe-2.0
%%EndProlog
/DataString 256 string def
0 1 255 {
        DataString exch dup put
} bind for
40 45 { pop } setscreen
72 72 scale 1 256 8 [1 0 0 256 0 0] {DataString} image
showpage
```

The spot function in this case consists only of a **pop** operation. The function is called with the stack holding the *x* and *y* coordinates (with *y* on top) of a position within the halftone cell. The **pop** removes the *y* coordinate from the stack so that the priority of any position in the halftone cell is its *x* coordinate. That is, the further to the right a position is within the halftone cell, the higher its *x* coordinate and the sooner the printer will print a spot at that position.

figure 8.4

-.8	-.4	0	.4	.8
-.8	-.4	0	.4	.8
-.8	-.4	0	.4	.8
-.8	-.4	0	.4	.8
-.8	-.4	0	.4	.8

The resulting priorities for a 5-by-5 halftone cell (the default in many PostScript interpreters) are shown in *figure 8.4*. These priorities render gray areas as a series of lines of varying thicknesses. The gradual blackening of the halftone cell is performed pixel by pixel by the PostScript interpreter, with pixels of highest priority (as determined by this spot function) being blackened first as the gray level is varied from white to black.

chapter 9

COMPLEX GRAPHIC PROBLEM-SOLVING

*If the only tool you have is a hammer,
you tend to see every problem as a nail.*

– *Anon.*

9.1 INTRODUCTION

This chapter focuses on some of the more complex graphic imaging problems that may be encountered when implementing a driver for a graphics application.

Some of the topics covered in this chapter involve graphic operations that are not indigenous to the PostScript imaging model. Nonetheless, there are graphics applications that need to render these effects on PostScript printers. Emphasis is placed on the most efficient methods for solving these graphics problems with the standard PostScript language imaging model.

9.2 PATTERN FILLS

Filling a region with a particular pattern currently presents some difficulty in the PostScript language. The **fill** operator invokes the halftone mechanism to fill a region with some particular color, but the halftone machinery is not intended for generalized pattern fills. In particular, halftone screens are rendered directly in device space, which makes it difficult to make the screens device-independent.

The halftone mechanism is the fastest method of providing a pattern fill as long as the pattern is not changed frequently. Since the halftone screen is intended to be set once and forgotten, much of the overhead is done when **setscreen** is invoked. Even if only one gray level is needed, they may all be computed (by calling the spot function as many times as necessary to build each possible halftone cell). This makes it fairly expensive to change the halftone screen. Halftone screens are also very device-dependent by nature, and do not rotate or scale with the current transformation matrix. Also, the screens are oriented in device space, and they probably will not work the same way on different devices.

Another approach to pattern fills is to use a *pattern font*. A character (or a number of characters) in a font may be defined to represent the fill pattern, and a region may be "tiled" by showing text within the boundaries of the region. Unfortunately, under most circumstances this requires use of the **clip** operator to establish the boundaries of the region to be filled before the pattern text is painted. This presents two difficulties:

- Clipping can be quite slow if the clipping region is complex (the region to be filled with a pattern, in this case).

- The available path space can overflow when **clip** is used on a complex path (yielding a **limitcheck** error).

However, the pattern font provides a general solution to device-independent pattern fills, and is a recommended approach.

In *listing 9-1* are some sample PostScript procedures which implement pattern filling algorithms. The approach is to define a font with pattern characters in it, then select one of those characters for tiling. The actual fill process uses **clip** to establish a clipping region, then uses **show** with rows of pattern characters to tile the area. Care is taken to assure that the pattern will lock into device space. This keeps the pattern from scaling or rotating, and helps guarantee that there will be no stitching problems between rows of the pattern.

listing 9-1

```
%!PS-Adobe-2.0
%%Title: patternfill.ps
%%EndComments
%%BeginProcSet: patternfill 1.0 0
```

```
% width height matrix proc key cache
% definepattern -> font
/definepattern { %def
    7 dict begin
        /FontDict 9 dict def
        FontDict begin
            /cache exch def
            /key exch def
            /proc exch cvx def
            /mtx exch matrix invertmatrix def
            /height exch def
            /width exch def
            /ctm matrix currentmatrix def
            /ptm matrix identmatrix def
            /str
            (123456789012345678901234567890 12)
            def
        end
        /FontBBox [ %def
            0 0 FontDict /width get
            FontDict /height get
        ] def
        /FontMatrix FontDict /mtx get def
        /Encoding StandardEncoding def
        /FontType 3 def
        /BuildChar { %def
            pop begin
            FontDict begin
                width 0 cache { %ifelse
                    0 0 width height setcachedevice
                }{ %else
                    setcharwidth
                } ifelse
                0 0 moveto width 0 lineto
                width height lineto 0 height lineto
                closepath clip newpath
                gsave proc grestore
            end end
        } def
        FontDict /key get currentdict definefont
    end
} bind def
```

```
% dict patternpath -
% dict matrix patternpath -
/patternpath { %def
    dup type /dicttype eq { %ifelse
        begin FontDict /ctm get setmatrix
    }{ %else
        exch begin FontDict /ctm get setmatrix
        concat
    } ifelse
    currentdict setfont
    FontDict begin
        FontMatrix concat
        width 0 dtransform
        round width div exch round width div exch
        0 height dtransform
        round height div exch
        round height div exch
        0 0 transform round exch round exch
        ptm astore setmatrix

        pathbbox
        height div ceiling height mul 4 1 roll
        width div ceiling width mul 4 1 roll
        height div floor height mul 4 1 roll
        width div floor width mul 4 1 roll

        2 index sub height div ceiling cvi exch
        3 index sub width div ceiling cvi exch
        4 2 roll moveto

        FontMatrix ptm invertmatrix pop
        { %repeat
            gsave
                ptm concat
                dup str length idiv { %repeat
                    str show
                } repeat
                dup str length mod str exch
                0 exch getinterval show
            grestore
            0 height rmoveto
        } repeat
        pop
    end end
} bind def
```

```
% dict patternfill -
% dict matrix patternfill -
/patternfill { %def
    gsave
        clip patternpath
    grestore
    newpath
} bind def

% dict patterneofill -
% dict matrix patterneofill -
/patterneofill { %def
    gsave
        eoclip patternpath
    grestore
    newpath
} bind def

% dict patternstroke -
% dict matrix patternstroke -
/patternstroke { %def
    gsave
        strokepath clip patternpath
    grestore
    newpath
} bind def

% dict ax ay string patternashow -
% dict matrix ax ay string patternashow -
/patternashow { %def
    (0) exch { %forall
        2 copy 0 exch put pop dup
        false charpath
        currentpoint
        5 index type /dicttype eq { %ifelse
            5 index patternfill
        }{ %else
            6 index 6 index patternfill
        } ifelse
        moveto
        3 copy pop rmoveto
    } forall
    pop pop pop
    dup type /dicttype ne { pop } if pop
} bind def
```

```
% dict string patternshow -
% dict matrix string patternshow -
/patternshow { %def
        0 exch 0 exch patternashow
} bind def

/opaquepatternfill { %def
        gsave
        1 setgray
        fill
        grestore
        patternfill
} bind def

/square { %def
        gsave
            moveto
            dup 0 rlineto
            dup 0 exch rlineto
            neg 0 rlineto
            closepath
            findfont  % a pattern font
            patternfill
        grestore
} bind def
%%EndProcSet
%%EndProlog


%%BeginSetup
15 15 [300 72 div 0 0 300 72 div 0 0]
{ %definepattern
        2 setlinecap
        7.5 0 moveto 15 7.5 lineto
        0 7.5 moveto 7.5 15 lineto
        2 setlinewidth stroke
} bind
/RIGHTdiagonal true definepattern pop

15 15 [300 72 div 0 0 300 72 div 0 0]
{ %definepattern
        2 setlinecap
        7.5 0 moveto 0 7.5 lineto
        15 7.5 moveto 7.5 15 lineto
        2 setlinewidth stroke
} bind
/LEFTdiagonal true definepattern pop
```

chapter 9 COMPLEX GRAPHIC PROBLEM-SOLVING

```
30 30 [300 72 div 0 0 300 72 div 0 0]
{ %definepattern
        2 2 scale
        2 setlinecap
        7.5 0 moveto 15 7.5 lineto
        0 7.5 moveto 7.5 15 lineto
        7.5 0 moveto 0 7.5 lineto
        15 7.5 moveto 7.5 15 lineto
        0.5 setlinewidth stroke
} bind
/crosshatch true definepattern pop

%%EndSetup
%%Page: 1 1
 /RIGHTdiagonal 72 460 100 square
 /LEFTdiagonal 72 480 120 square
 /crosshatch 72 500 140 square
 showpage
%%Trailer
```

9.3   LOGOS, GRIDS, FORMS, AND SPECIAL FONTS

It is often desirable to create a graphic object that will be printed on every page of a document, such as a company logotype, a
printed form (like an income tax form), or perhaps a background grid of some sort. Depending on the complexity of the
image, this can be accomplished in one of several ways.

The first (and simplest) approach to this problem is to place the
necessary PostScript code to draw the image into a procedure,
and to invoke the procedure at the start of each page. This is the
most general solution, and if the complexity of the image is not
too great, this is the best approach. *Listing 9-2* provides a procedure that will produce a simple logotype.

The start of each page can then begin with an invocation of this
logo procedure. This will help save the transmission and scanning overhead for each page, but the object will still need to be
executed on each page.

listing 9-2 ————————————

```
%!PS-Adobe-1.0
%%Title: logo procedure
%%EndComments
/logo { %def
        % draw at current point
    gsave
        /Times-Roman findfont
        48 scalefont setfont
        (G) show -13.5 -14.5 rmoveto (R) show
    grestore
    -4 -8 rmoveto
    /Helvetica findfont 11 scalefont setfont
    (glenn) show 22 3 rmoveto (reid) show
} bind def
%%EndProlog
gsave
        100 100 moveto logo
grestore
showpage
%%Trailer
```

The **copypage** operator is designed to print the current page without disturbing the contents of the frame buffer into which the page has been imaged. This permits reusing the image that already exists on the page. A form of "electronic mask white" may be used from one page to the next to erase the fields on the form and print new data in those areas. (This can be accomplished simply by setting the current color to white and using **fill**.)

The only difficulty with using **copypage** is that it doesn't allow fast PostScript interpreters to take advantage of parallel processing. In most implementations of the PostScript interpreter there is a provision for writing bits into one part of the frame buffer while the other end is being imaged onto paper. In extremely fast printers there may be many different frame buffers and a high degree of parallel processing. If the user program forces reuse of the same frame buffer by using **copypage**, this parallelism may be defeated (and the printer will run much slower than its rated capacity). There is a trade-off between using **copypage** and executing the procedure on each page. The use of **copypage** is discouraged in all but the most unusual situations.

The third approach that can be used to create a reusable graphic image is to make it a character in a *user-defined font*. The font may contain only a single character, or perhaps many such images. Each image is simply a procedure that is invoked by the font machinery as if to draw a character shape. The advantage of this method is that if the image is an appropriate size to fit into the font cache, then it will be extremely fast. In *listing 9-3* is the **logo** procedure from the *listing 9-2*, placed into font format and invoked by a single-character **show** operation:

listing 9-3 ————————————————————————————

```
%!PS-Adobe-2.0
%%Title: logo font example
%%EndComments
/F { findfont exch scalefont setfont } bind def
%%EndProlog
%%BeginSetup
%%BeginFont: Logo-Font 1.0 0
 12 dict begin  % leave one empty slot for FID
     /FontName /Logo-Font def
     /FontMatrix [ 1 0 0 1 0 0 ] def
     /FontType 3 def
     /FontBBox [ -5 -12 85 50 ] def
     /BuildChar { %def
         exch begin
             70 0 -5 -12 85 50 setcachedevice
             Encoding exch get load exec
         end
 } bind def
 /Encoding 256 array %def
     dup 0 1 255 { /.notdef put dup } for pop
     dup 71 /logo put  % "G" character
 def
 /logo { %def
     % draw at current point
     20 0 moveto
```

```
      gsave
            /Times-Roman findfont
            48 scalefont setfont
            (G) show -13.5 -14.5 rmoveto (R) show
      grestore
      -4 -8 rmoveto
      /Helvetica findfont 11 scalefont setfont
      (glenn) show 22 3 rmoveto (reid) show
   } bind def
currentdict end
dup /FontName get exch definefont pop
%%EndFont: Logo-Font
%%EndSetup
%%Page: 1 1
  gsave
        100 100 moveto
        1.5 /Logo-Font F (G) show
  grestore
  showpage
%%Trailer
```

GRIDS

Producing a grid of lines can result in some slightly unexpected results, due to the rounding of line widths as lines are stroked. (See also Section 5.4.) The following sequence produces a thin line on the page:

```
.1 setlinewidth
72 72 moveto
572 72 lineto
stroke
```

However, the exact thickness of the line depends on where the **moveto** and **lineto** coordinates fall in device space. PostScript maintains the full precision of coordinates all the way through to device space, and it is not until the execution of **stroke** or **fill** that decisions are made for painting individual device pixels. *Figure 9.1* is an illustration with a **moveto lineto stroke** sequence for a short line segment. It shows the interior of the stroked path and the pixels that are blackened by **stroke**.

figure 9.1

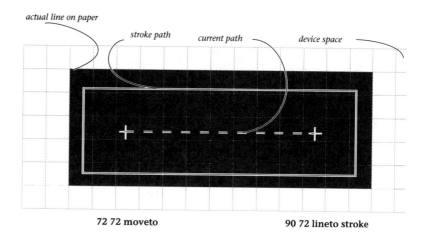

actual line on paper stroke path current path device space

72 72 moveto **90 72 lineto stroke**

Two procedures are defined in *listing 9-4* (redefinitions of the **moveto** and **lineto** operators) that provide lines of uniform thickness, although their spacing cannot also be guaranteed. The crux of these procedures is the use of the **transform** and **itransform** operators.

The coordinates for **moveto** and **lineto** are actually transformed into device space and rounded off to the nearest device pixel boundary. The coordinates are then inverse-transformed back into user space, and the subsequent **moveto** or **lineto** is executed. The points are then guaranteed to land on pixel boundaries, which will cause **stroke** to produce a line of a uniform thickness regardless of where on the page the lines are located.

Notice that the coordinates in device space are not inspected in any way; they are merely rounded off and returned to user space. This keeps the code from becoming device-dependent, since no assumptions are made as to the resolution.

Figure 9.2 shows the line that results when the **M** and **L** procedures are used instead of **moveto** and **lineto**. Since the locations are rounded to the nearest device pixel, the **stroke** operation always encompasses the same number of pixels to either side of the path, resulting in an even line.

listing 9-4 ————————————————————————

```
%!PS-Adobe-2.0
%%Title: line thickness example
%%EndComments
/M { %def
    transform
    round exch round exch
    itransform
    moveto
} bind def
/L { %def
    transform
    round exch round exch
    itransform
    lineto
} bind def
%%EndProlog
gsave
    .1 setlinewidth
    10 10 800 { %for
        pop 0 10 translate
        550 0 M  612 0 L
        stroke
    } bind for
grestore
showpage
%%Trailer
```

figure 9.2

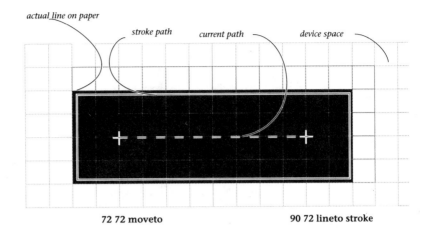

actual line on paper   stroke path   current path   device space

72 72 moveto   90 72 lineto stroke

9.4 TRANSFORMATION MATRICES

Coordinate system transformations, including **translate**, **rotate**, **scale**, and **concat**, are *matrix operations* that affect the current transformation matrix that exists between user coordinate space and device coordinate space. This mapping is represented by a six-element array (or matrix). All coordinate system transformations are combined with the existing transformation simply by multiplying the existing matrix by the elements of the new transformation.

Scaling and translating are easy. There are specific elements of the matrix which directly affect these operations:

[*Xscale 0 0 Yscale Xtranslate Ytranslate*]

In the following code fragments, the first line in each pair is equivalent to the second line in the pair:

3 5 scale
[3 0 0 5 0 0] concat

100 300 translate
[1 0 0 1 100 300] concat

100 200 translate 2 2 scale
[2 0 0 2 100 200] concat

The **concat** operator allows you to supply a complete matrix which is to be concatenated with the existing transformation matrix. Each of the **scale** and **translate** operations in the previous example is easily represented by specifying the appropriate matrix and using **concat**. The **scale**, **rotate**, and **translate** operators are provided for convenience, but are not strictly necessary.

Rotation of the coordinate space is less straightforward. The entries in the matrix are actually derived by taking the **sin** or **cos** of the desired angle of rotation:

[cos*(angle)* sin*(angle)* -sin*(angle)* cos*(angle)* 0 0]

The following is an example of the combined effects of translation and rotation. In order to set "landscape" mode, the coordinate axes must be rotated 90 degrees and translated so that the origin remains in the lower left-hand corner of the page. Both of the following PostScript segments will place a standard "letter" sized paper in landscape mode:

90 rotate
0 -612 translate

612 0 translate
90 rotate

Notice that in both cases the sequence **90 rotate** is used, but the translation component is *not* the same.

Note:

> *These coordinate system transformations are not commutative. That is, if the order of evaluation is changed, different results may be achieved. By convention, landscape pages should always be effected by first rotating (positive angle) then translating (negative Y value):*

90 rotate   0 -612 translate

As a convention, it is best always to accomplish rotation of a page into a landscape orientation in this manner (*positive* 90 degrees for the rotation component, then a *negative* translation component along the Y axis). This is so that if the page is nested in another page or scaled, the landscape orientation can be preserved easily.

INVERTED COORDINATE SYSTEMS

It is possible to *invert* the coordinate system so that positive *y* values grow downward, for instance. This particular transformation can be accomplished as follows:

0 792 translate % top of page
1 -1 scale

This moves the origin to the upper left corner of the (letter-sized) page, and "flips" the *y* axis. Note that although graphics can be easily inverted this way, text requires some special attention to keep it from being inverted, as well. One way to address this is to use the **makefont** operator instead of **scalefont**:

/Times-Roman findfont
[12 0 0 -12 0 0] makefont setfont

The **-12** in the scale matrix inverts the text about the *y* axis, which will counteract the inversion of the entire user space coordinate system, causing the text to be right-side up.

Inverting the coordinate system is a specialized approach, and probably should be used only when it is difficult or impossible to use the standard orientation.

9.5 COLOR AND COLOR SEPARATIONS

Printing in color using the PostScript language model provides some very powerful capabilities. Colors can be specified with a reflectance model using percentages of using *cyan*, *magenta*, *yellow*, and *black* (using the **setcmykcolor** operator), which correspond to the four colors used in full process color printing. Color can also be specified using a *luminance model*, using either the *hue*, *saturation*, and *brightness* model (with the **sethsbcolor** operator) or the *red, green, blue* color model (using the **setrgbcolor** operator).

For color printing, the reflectance model is generally used, with cyan, magenta, yellow, and black as the component colors. Color PostScript printers provide direct support for this color model through the **setcmykcolor** operator and through related operators to control four separate halftone screens and transfer functions. A **colorimage** operator is also provided for rendering full color images.

Once a color has been specified in the user program, it is rendered through a PostScript language abstraction similar to the black-and-white halftoning mechanism. A current color is established in the graphics state, and all the painting operators use the current color as they apply paint to the current page. The PostScript language interpreter is responsible for producing that color on a given output device. If the device is a screen, the color must be displayed through available screen phosphors. With color printing devices, the color may be produced by successive passes of cyan, magenta, yellow, and black, where each pass uses the appropriate percentage of color as specified by the user program.

COLOR SEPARATIONS

If a PostScript program contains color specification, it can be printed on any PostScript interpreter, and the device will render the color to the best of its ability. However, for full process color presses, you may wish to separate the image into its four components of cyan, magenta, yellow, and black. This can be done by producing four photographic masters (camera-ready plates), one for each process color. These plates are actually printed in black and white using the standard halftoning mechanism, and each plate is then overprinted with the appropriate process color ink in the final press run.

Color separations may be obtained simply by redefining the color operators to essentially throw away all but a single process color. The file must then be printed in four passes, where each pass sifts out a different process color. (See *listing 9-5*.)

listing 9-5 ——————————

```
%!PS-Adobe-2.0
%%Title: separation.ps
/separations 24 dict def
separations begin
    /cmykprocs [ %def
    % cyan
        { pop pop pop 1 exch sub setgray }
    % magenta
        { pop pop exch pop 1 exch sub setgray }
    % yellow
        { pop 3 1 roll pop pop 1 exch sub setgray }
    % black
        { 4 1 roll pop pop pop 1 exch sub setgray }
    ] def
    /screenangles [ %def
        105  % cyan
        75   % magenta
        0    % yellow
        45   % black
    ] def
end  % separations
% setupcolor takes 0, 1, 2, or 3 as its argument,
% for cyan, magenta, yellow, and black.
/CYAN 0 def          /MAGENTA 1 def
/YELLOW 2 def        /BLACK 3 def
/setupcolor { %def
    userdict begin
        dup separations /cmykprocs get exch get
        /setcmykcolor exch def
        separations /screenangles get exch get
        currentscreen
            exch pop 3 -1 roll exch
        setscreen
        /setscreen { pop pop pop } def
    end
} bind def
%%EndProlog
%%BeginSetup
 CYAN setupcolor
%%EndSetup
%%BeginDocument: originalfile.ps
        % entire file is placed here.
%%EndDocument
%%Trailer
```

The halftone screen angles used are extremely important to good color separations. Each process color component should be printed with a different screen angle to minimize color interference in the final press run. The exact angles used are device-dependent and should be determined separately for each different PostScript device. The goal is to provide placement of color spots that will not interfere with one another, and which will avoid moiré patterns as the screens are overlaid.

SPOT COLOR

Spot color is much different than four-color process printing. If you imagine real printing presses, the kind you put ink into instead of toner, you can imagine using a colored ink instead of using black. That is a good model of spot color. It is a single color of ink, rather than a color that is composed as some mix of the four process colors cyan, magenta, yellow, and black.

There are two sides of spot color: specifying the color and actually printing it. If and when there are devices which permit printing with two or three (or more) individual colors on a single device, then those colors must be specified by the user program in much the same way that shades of gray are specified with the **setgray** operator. More commonly, spot color will be mastered on a black-and-white device and printed on a high-speed press with colored inks. From the PostScript interpreter's point of view, it will be printing only in shades of black, although the masters may eventually be printed with a colored ink when taken to press.

Probably the simplest way to specify spot color is to be able to selectively print components of a document. For example, if a user decides that all chapter headings in a book are to be printed in a particular color of green, and the rest of the book is to be printed in black, he or she needs some way to print the document in two individual passes: the green pass and the black pass. To produce the green pass, only those objects in the document which are specified as green should be printed at all (the black material is simply not printed).

An application program can permit "tagging" of objects to be one color or another, and provide a mechanism for printing only selected objects by naming them. In this way the user can selectively print some part of the document to obtain a separation. The PostScript interpreter, of course, is simply interpreting and printing graphics in some shade of black or white, and nothing at all is required at the PostScript level.

If the application produces PostScript code that is sufficiently modular, each graphic element on the page can be bracketed by the special comments %%BeginObject and %%EndObject. These comments simply provide a way to name the graphic elements on the page. A post-processing program could then selectively extract certain elements of the page for printing. (See the *PostScript Document Structuring Conventions* document from Adobe Systems for more information on these comments).

The PostScript imaging model, however, can complicate the real world of spot color. For instance, if a black rectangle is drawn and filled and a green circle is printed on top of it, the PostScript imaging model completely overwrites the black with the green. However, if the page is printed in two passes, with one pass containing only the black elements and the other pass only the green ones, the black rectangle will not have a white circle cut out of it where the green will go. When green ink is actually printed on top of the black ink on a regular press, some muddying of the color will result. To be done correctly, the black pass should have color *removed* wherever another color would be overlaid on top of it. This is a much more difficult thing to accomplish, and cannot be done by simply printing individual page elements selectively.

This kind of separation problem can also occur in four-color process printing, if the overlaid colors are printed without first removing any colors which may precede them.

This nuance of color printing can be accommodated at the PostScript language level simply by redefining some of the color specification operators. Rather than extracting and printing individual objects on a page, all of them may be sent to the printer. To print a separation, the color operators are redefined to print black wherever, say, green is specified, and to print with *white* if any other color is called for. Then, in any place where the green would be obscured by another color above it, that second color would be printed in white, effectively erasing that part of the green image. The technique for this is much like that found in *listing 9-5*. The difference is the selection process—rather than selecting only the cyan pass, some method of selection by name must be implemented in order to specify the spot color. The full details of this specification and separation technique are beyond the scope of this book. For more detailed information, please contact someone at Adobe Systems.

chapter 10

FILE INTERCHANGE STANDARDS

*Many of the greatest things man has achieved
are not the result of consciously directed thought,
and still less the product of a deliberately coordinated effort
of many individuals, but of a process in which the individual
plays a part which he can never fully understand.*

– Friedrich August von Hayek

10.1 INTRODUCTION

PostScript language print files that are intended to migrate between different environments should observe standard structuring conventions, and they should be device independent. The standardized structure permits document managers to incorporate the documents into other systems and to print them in the appropriate environment. It also makes parallel processing possible and provides a mechanism for ensuring that fonts and other resources are supplied as needed.

10.2 CONFORMING DOCUMENTS

A *conforming document* is a PostScript document file that correctly observes the structuring conventions. There are two aspects to a conforming document file:

- *Comments:* The structure of the file should be delineated (as appropriate) by structure comment conventions. These are PostScript comments in a specific format that can be parsed by applications software to determine the structure and contents of a PostScript file. (See Section 6.4.) The comments include an introductory comment that marks a file as a conforming file (including a version number).

- *Structure:* The structure of the file should be in conformance with the file structuring guidelines. This includes page modularity (pages should be functionally independent) and the avoidance (or careful use) of system-level PostScript language operators such as **initgraphics** and **erasepage**.

The rules for conformance are not particularly limiting. Conforming files are, for the most part, ordinary PostScript language program files. The notion of conformance is introduced as a guarantee to applications software that the file plays by the rules.

10.3   HANDLING PRINTER-SPECIFIC FEATURES

In order for PostScript language files to be truly portable, any code that invokes a specific device attribute (such as a paper tray or frame buffer) must be clearly segregated in the structure of the file. Print file managers (or "spoolers") can take action to replace a device-dependent module from a program file, but only if these sections can be identified easily.

In order to provide a general mechanism for invoking printer-specific features, Adobe Systems has provided *PostScript Printer Description Files*, which collectively set forth a machine-parsable file format containing a representation for the PostScript program fragments needed to invoke particular features on each printer. These files are arranged by *keywords* for each feature, and document management software can easily extract the necessary PostScript language fragment to set a paper tray, invoke manual feed, or determine whether or not a certain font is present in ROM.

Document composition software should produce a PostScript document file that contains an indication of what printer-specific features are needed (or what features have been invoked in that file already, and might need to be changed if the file is sent to a different printer). This indication is in the form of PostScript language comments:

```
%%BeginPaperSize: Ledger
statusdict begin
    ledgertray
end
%%EndPaperSize
```

This PostScript language sequence correctly invokes the **ledger-tray** operator on any printer that has this operator in **status-dict**. If a document manager wishes to send the file to a different printer than was originally intended (that may have a slightly different method for invoking the **Ledger** paper size), it should remove the code between these comments, and use the keyword **Ledger** to find the appropriate PostScript language segment from the printer description file, with which it will replace the previous code sequence. Even if it happens to be sent to another printer for which **ledgertray** is the appropriate operator, it doesn't hurt to replace it.

10.4   SPECIFYING PAPER SIZES

Formatting a document is different from printing a document. A document formatting program makes decisions about where page elements will fall on the printed page. However, in the PostScript language imaging model, the document formatter lays pages out in user space. It is easy enough to modify the mapping between user space and device space to achieve almost any kind of printing need.

Because of this flexibility in printing, there are really two different decisions that need to be made to choose a page size. The first decision is made when the PostScript print file is formatted. If the intended page size is, say, 11 by 17 inches (ledger paper), then the numbers in the PostScript file address user space coordinates anywhere from 0 to 1224 in the x direction. Let us draw a simple box around the intended page to illustrate this. The box represents a collection of marks that could be an entire document on ledger-size paper. The important thing is to have coordinates in the program that are in the range of 1224 in the x direction. (See *listing 10-1.*) Notice the use of the comments to provide information about the program, especially the **%%BoundingBox** comment.

listing 10-1 _____

```
%!PS-Adobe-2.0
%%BoundingBox: 0 0 1224 792
%
% <width> <height> <llX> <llY> <thick> box
/box { %def
    gsave
        setlinewidth moveto
        dup 0 exch rlineto
        exch 0 rlineto
        0 exch neg rlineto
        closepath stroke
    grestore
} bind def
%%EndProlog
1152 720 36 36 3 box
showpage
%%Trailer
```

This program prints a rectangular border (with a line thickness of 3 points) one half inch in each direction from the edges of an 11-by-17 inch page. The rectangle is 10 inches high and 16 inches long. The coordinates in this file represent a decision to lay out the box on a ledger-sized sheet of paper, in a sense.

The second decision is to print the document. Notice the distinction between the composition of the document and the act of printing it. At this stage, a particular printer is chosen. It is typical to inspect a proof of the document on the screen first, then perhaps on a medium-resolution printer, and use a high resolution image-setter for final output. Each device may have a different capability for rendering a page size as large as 11 x 17 (including, perhaps, not being able to support it at all).

The actual invocation of a specific paper size should be done *at print time*. In *listing 10-2* is the same example with specific printing instructions added. In particular, the **ledgertray** operator is invoked to print on 11-by-17 inch paper. This code is put between a **%%BeginPaperSize** and **%%EndPaperSize** comment since the code is (by necessity) device dependent.

listing 10-2 ——————————————————————

```
%!PS-Adobe-2.0
%%BoundingBox: 0 0 1224 792
%%DocumentPaperSizes: Ledger
%%EndComments
% <width> <height> <llX> <llY> <thick> box
 /box { %def
   gsave
       setlinewidth moveto
       dup 0 exch rlineto
       exch 0 rlineto
       0 exch neg rlineto
       closepath stroke
   grestore
 } bind def
%%EndProlog
%%BeginSetup
%%BeginPaperSize: Ledger
 statusdict begin
/ledgertray where { %ifelse
       pop ledgertray
 }{ %else
       90 rotate 0 -612 translate
       792 1224 div dup scale
       % scale down for proofing on letter paper
 } ifelse
 end
%%EndPaperSize
%%EndSetup
%%Page: 1 1
 1152 720 36 36 3 box
 showpage
%%Trailer
```

Notice that the PaperSize code checks for the existence of the **ledgertray** operator (using the **where** operator) and if it is not found, the page is printed much smaller to fit on letter-size paper. This technique can help provide fallbacks for devices which may not contain the required features (see also Section 10.6).

10.5 PRINTER QUERIES

A PostScript language printer has the capability of providing a great deal of information back to the host computer. After all, PostScript is a complete programming language with full input/output support across the communications channel. However, the process of issuing a query to a PostScript interpreter can present some difficulties.

A *query* is defined to be a PostScript program whose sole purpose is to return some information from the PostScript interpreter back to the host computer. An example of this might be a short program to enumerate the names of all the fonts currently stored in the printer. Queries are typically issued even before the print file is produced, since some decisions may have to be made based on the available paper sizes and on the resident fonts. In an interactive environment, the notion of a query is a little less strict, since virtually every transaction will provide some information back to the host application.

By querying the printer (or more generally, the PostScript interpreter), information can be obtained about the state of the interpreter. However, if the issuing software *expects* a particular bit of returned information, it may become impossible to introduce a print spooler between the composition software and the printer (unless the spooler could somehow interpret and answer the queries). See Chapter 12 for more details on writing print spoolers for PostScript interpreters.

Since the need for querying is acknowledged under some circumstances, a specific protocol has been establish whereby queries are isolated into a single job, followed by an end-of-file indication. In addition, the queries should have well-formed PostScript comments to provide information to spoolers as to the nature of the query. In any case, the queries should be kept to an absolute minimum. *Listing 10-3* is an example of a query job (two individual queries are contained within the job). Notice the first line of the file, which contains a special notation to identify the job as a query job:

%!PS-Adobe-2.0 **Query**

This is so that software reading the comments can quickly ascertain that it is a query job. See the *PostScript Document Structuring Conventions* for more detail on this.

listing 10-3 ──────────────────────────

```
%!PS-Adobe-2.0 Query
%%Title: sample query job
%%?BeginFontQuery: Palatino-Roman
/Palatino-Roman
dup FontDirectory exch known { %ifelse
      1  % yes
}{
      0  % no
} ifelse == flush pop
%%?EndFontQuery
%%?BeginVMStatus
 vmstatus exch sub == flush pop
%%?EndVMStatus
%%EOF
```

10.6 CONDITIONAL EXECUTION

When invoking a PostScript operator that may not be present in all implementations, it is best to put it in a context of *conditional execution*. This way the program can provide a reasonable alternative if the feature is not present on a given printer. For example, *listing 10-4* is an invocation of the ledger-size paper tray that prints the page scaled down on letter-size paper if ledger is not available.

listing 10-4 ──────────────────────────

```
%!PS-Adobe-2.0
%%EndComments
%%EndProlog
%%BeginSetup
%%BeginPaperSize: Ledger
 statusdict /ledgertray known { %if
```

```
      statusdict begin
          ledgertray
      end
  }{ %else
      (Ledger not found. Scaling...\n) print
      792 1224 div dup scale
  } ifelse
%%EndPaperSize
%%EndSetup
%%Page: 1 1
 showpage
%%Trailer
```

10.7   FONT AVAILABILITY

One of the most common difficulties encountered when port-
ing PostScript files from one environment to another is the
availability of fonts. If a document is composed to be printed
with a particular font, it basically should not be printed at all if
the font is unavailable (there are some circumstances under
which font substitution is appropriate—see Chapter 4 for more
on this).

A document file should communicate its font needs to other
software through PostScript structure comments. There are a
number of comments which may apply when fonts are used:

```
%%DocumentFonts: Optima StoneSans Courier
%%DocumentNeededFonts: Optima
%%DocumentSuppliedFonts: StoneSans
%%EndComments
  ...
%%IncludeFont: Optima
  ...
%%BeginFont: StoneSans
 % font description here
%%EndFont
```

The **%%DocumentFonts** comment provides a list of all the
fonts that are actually referenced in the document (a **findfont**

is done). The **%%DocumentNeededFonts** comment is used to indicate that there is explicit use of the **%%IncludeFont** comment. It is an indication that the file should be parsed to satisfy a font request embedded in the file. The **%%DocumentSupplied-Fonts** comment is used where an entire font description is contained within the body of the document file (as a downloadable font). The font itself is delimited by **%%BeginFont** and **%%EndFont** comments, as in the example. Again, the header comment is provided for information about what is contained in the body of the file.

When a file is imported, either from another system or as an illustration in a document, these comments should be parsed to determine the font needs of the document being imported. When appropriate, the importing application must locate the needed fonts and place them in-line in the file, and/or update its own structure comments to reflect the aggregate font needs of its own document file and the imported one.

10.8 PUTTING IT ALL TOGETHER

PostScript document files can have many complex requirements. This is partly because the possibilities are so rich, and because the PostScript language is complete. There are large sets of manuals provided for most programming environments with convention after convention that need to be followed for compatibility even with different versions of a single machine. The PostScript language spans many systems and architectures and the conventions for its use are correspondingly relatively simple. However, they are extremely important, in much the same way that all programming conventions are important: they help ensure compatibility across many kinds of products and environments. If they are observed properly, everyone benefits.

Here are some brief guidelines for structuring documents properly, and for using the conventions appropriately, and to reduce some of the complexity to simple rules of thumb:

- If a structuring convention or comment doesn't make sense in the environment that you are working in, don't use it. For example, omit the **%%BoundingBox** comment if you are issuing a query, and don't put in the **%%Page** comments if the pages aren't functionally independent of one another.

- If you include PostScript code that is not clearly documented as being a standard part of the language, then *mark this code* with some kind of **%%Begin** and **%%End** comments, according to the comment conventions.

- If the entire PostScript job is somehow special (a downloaded font, a query, or an **exitserver** job, for example), mark it at the beginning of the job according to the conventions.

- If you are unsure of whether your file is conforming, try importing it into another document as an illustration, and see if it works.

- Don't execute any of the initialization operators (any operator that contains **init** or **default**, among others).

- As a rule of thumb, don't execute anything in the prologue (including **save**), and don't define anything new in the script (unless it is a state variable).

- Don't try to put **save** and **restore** around your whole job, prologue and all. That is done for you. It also makes the file *non-conforming* if you do. Do put **save** and **restore** around the individual pages of the script, or even more frequently, if appropriate.

chapter 11

MERGING FILES
FROM DIFFERENT SOURCES

*Life being all inclusion and confusion, and
art being all discrimination and selection,
the latter, in search of the hard latent value
with which it alone is concerned, sniffs round the
mass as instinctively and unerringly as a
dog suspicious of some buried bone.*

– Henry James

11.1   INTRODUCTION

One goal of software integration is to be able to produce complex documents. For instance, a report may need to contain a graph of data stored in a company database. This involves integrating data into a graphics application and merging it with text. Often the result of this integration is a printed page or a transparency for an overhead presentation.

In a PostScript environment, this can be accomplished at print time in much the same way that photographs are added directly to the plates ("stripped in") for an offset printer. If the software used to produce the graphs can produce a PostScript file as output, it can be merged with the PostScript output from a word processor to print the graph on the same page as the text. Essentially, it means the ability to paste in illustrations composed by other software.

The nature of the PostScript language makes this work quite well. The coordinate system can be scaled and translated before the illustration is executed, and the entire graph can be printed at some percentage of its original size, and even rotated. However, some cooperation between the composing software and the importing software is necessary to allow it to work smoothly.

This chapter is devoted to the relationship that should exist between the composing software and the importing software. It is closely related to Chapter 10, in that the best way to successfully merge PostScript files from different sources is to make sure that all the files are conforming PostScript files.

11.2   USING EXISTING CONTEXT

Every PostScript program executes in the context of an already executing PostScript program. At the start, a print file executes within the context of the server loop, which is just another piece of code. Any given PostScript file may have another complete program file embedded within it, which then executes in whatever context is presented to it by the outer program.

In order to keep track of who is who, let us define some terms:

- *Document File:* The document file is a PostScript program that may have another program embedded within it. It is typically simply the output of a page layout program or other document-producing software.

- *Illustration:* This is a program which executes *within* the context of another PostScript program. It need not truly be an illustration, but it is a good way to think of the relationship.

- *Print Job:* This refers to the PostScript file that is at the outermost level of execution. Note that this does *not* include the server loop. It is the first user-level print file.

Every PostScript program should be written as though it were an illustration, even if it is printed directly rather than imported into another document. A document file and an illustration do not differ at the PostScript language level, except that an illustration typically will not consist of more than one page. They differ at the conceptual level and in terms of how they are being used. Please refer to Chapter 6 for more details on program modularity and independence.

A PostScript program should only change those elements of the ground state of the interpreter that are necessary for its own execution, and it should return the state of the interpreter to that same condition when it is through executing. The recovery can be accomplished simply by using **save** and **restore**, but it is the programmer's responsibility not to disturb any parts of the machine's state that do not need to be modified for the task at hand. In particular, it is important never to initialize the state of the interpreter.

11.3   ERROR RECOVERY

There is a discussion of error recovery principles in Chapter 14 of this book. In general, it is okay for a document program to merely report an error in a reasonable fashion, rather than being expected to recover from it gracefully. For instance, if a mechanism is put in place that assigns a job name to each illustration that is embedded in it, then any execution errors which might result from the execution of those files can be identified easily by that name. In some cases, a print job cannot do any better than this at error recovery. For instance, if the illustration is actually reading from the current file (as with the **image** operator), it may not quit reading at the appropriate place in the file (if it is not written correctly), and could read *past* the end of the illustration and into the rest of the original document.

The **stopped** operator can be used to catch (almost all) execution errors in an embedded illustration. In Chapter 14 (*listing 14-2*) there is a procedure called **userexec** which is used much like **exec**. It takes any executable object (for instance, the file object returned by **currentfile cvx**) and executes it in an error-recovery context. This can be used quite effectively for included illustrations, if needed. For most purposes, it is better to identify the included job by some name, and trust it to execute correctly. If it doesn't, the user will know what happened if you supply the name of the file that was executing when the error occurred.

11.4 HANDLING **SHOWPAGE**

Since the **showpage** operator is common to almost all PostScript programs, it is not fair to make it illegal in a conforming PostScript file. Instead, the burden is placed on the including document to disable **showpage** when appropriate. In *listing 11-1* is a bit of code that might be wrapped around a program file that is to be embedded into the current file.

listing 11-1 ———————————————————————————————

```
%!PS-Adobe-2.0
%%Title: include.ps
%%EndComments
%%BeginProcSet: include.ps 1.0 0
/beginexecute { %def
    /level0 save def
    /showpage { } def
    /jobname exch def
} bind def
/endexecute { %def
    level0 restore
} bind def
%%EndProcSet
%%EndProlog
% including "Illustration.ps"
(Illustration.ps) beginexecute
0 0 translate   % if needed
1 1 scale       % if needed
%%BeginDocument: Illustration.ps
%!PS-Adobe-2.0
%%Title: Illustration.ps
jobname = flush
%%Trailer
%%EndDocument
endexecute
showpage
%%Trailer
```

———————————————————————————————

This disables the **showpage** operator for the duration of the execution of "Illustration.ps," and reinstates it to its original value (whatever it may have been) after the **restore**. Notice also that the name of the file is made available in the **jobname** entry, which can be reported if an error occurs.

11.5 SCREEN REPRESENTATIONS

In visual page composition systems, it is typically possible to see on the screen what will eventually print. It is an unusual approach to be able to print what you cannot see (or edit). This situation arises whenever printing technology advances more rapidly than front-end composition systems. In general, it is powerful to build front-end systems that permit inclusion of unknown elements that are specific to the printing technology (a bit image, perhaps).

In most environments, some indication must be given on the host system wherever an imported file is added by the application. As a specific example, a visual page layout program may have the capability to merge a PostScript file into the output from the program, but it needs some mechanism for representing the image on the front end.

There are three approaches to this problem. The first is the simplest, and the last is probably the best:

1. *Represent the included file by name.* One example of this is simply an "include" statement in the input file:

   #include "illustration.ps"

   In a markup-language approach to document layout, this is usually the way files are included. A slightly more sophisticated approach might include displaying a rectangle on the screen where the drawing will be placed (or permitting it to be scaled or moved on the page as it is being imported).

2. *Display a simulated bit image* of the illustration on the screen, but do not print it (send the PostScript file to the printer instead). This simulated image could be prepared by the software that produced the illustration in

the first place, and must be represented by a convention to which each application agrees.

3. *Interpret the PostScript Code.* If the PostScript file can be executed and displayed directly, no simulation is required. This can be thought of as a "preview" capability if the software does not use the PostScript language as its display model already.

In each of these approaches, the importing application can handle the file better if it knows that it is a PostScript language illustration. In particular, it can consult the *bounding box* information in the file to display the appropriate rectangle, or it can display the simulated bit image on the screen if it knows where to look for it.

A current convention in the industry is for a drawing application to produce conforming PostScript files with a "preview" bit image along with them, in a standard format which importing applications can understand. It is then up to the importing program to display the bit image on the screen and keep the PostScript program to send to the printer.

As the PostScript language becomes more commonplace for screen drivers, the applications may not need to use the previewed bit image stored with the file, but may choose to interpret the PostScript code directly.

chapter 12

WRITING A
PRINT SPOOLER

12.1 INTRODUCTION

A *print spooler* is a program that collects output for a given printer or network and saves it for later printing. The file may then be put in line behind others waiting to print, or it may be printed immediately, but the host application which originally sent the print job can return to what it was doing, knowing that the job has been queued (or has printed) successfully.

The advantages of this mechanism are well known. A job may be reprinted or rescheduled, it may be cancelled, and (best of all) the host application doesn't have to wait for it to print.

The difficulties result from the fact that the link between the application and the printer is made more indirect. Certainly a front-end program that tries to query the printer to find out about available resources would be surprised if the device did not answer. Also, the possibility arises that a job might be queued for one printer but be actually printed on another device.

Cooperation is required, as usual, on both ends of an exchange like this. The host applications must behave appropriately so that they do not make assumptions about the printer that would make it difficult or impossible to write a print spooler. The spooler must be written in such a way that it is completely transparent—if the job would have printed without the spooler, it should print through the spooler as well.

The assumptions in this chapter apply almost exclusively to PostScript interpreters in batch mode. Any interactive systems will probably not use print spoolers.

12.2 PRINTER MANAGEMENT

PostScript is a programming language. It is conceivable that a one-line program sent to a standard PostScript interpreter could cause 2 megabytes of information to be sent back to the host computer. This is (today) a little unusual for a printer. In some instances, it is a temptation: "Why should I take the time to compute something that the printer already knows; I'll just ask the printer." In other instances, the information may be a part of the standard communication with the printer (for instance, if an execution error occurs, an error message is sent back to the host system).

The task of *managing* a PostScript printer is a larger issue than simply print spooling. There are resource management issues (is *Optima* a resident font, is it on the printer's local disk, is it available on a font server, or should it be downloaded?). Handling and reporting errors, out-of-paper conditions, and paper jams is the responsibility of the printer management software. Perhaps print job arbitration and file spooling is another function of this software, although they are usually separate entities.

12.3 COMMUNICATIONS

The low-level considerations of maintaining two-way communication with a PostScript device are a critical part of printer management. There are some aspects of this communication which differ greatly from other printing devices, and which need attention in the design phase.

The batch job model under which PostScript printers normally operate is founded on individual print files. That is, a single job is defined from the initial byte through the final end-of-file indication. The end-of-file (EOF) should *never* be contained in the document file itself; it is part of the communication dynamics. In fact, the EOF marker for, say, a serial port is much different than the EOF indication on a packet network.

The PostScript interpreter will *echo* an EOF to match each EOF that it receives. This is a confirmation that the entire file has been received. A second job should never be sent until the first one has completely finished executing (including echoing back the EOF indication).

MESSAGES

PostScript printers tend to generate ASCII text messages back to the host system. Some of these are in response to status requests, and some of them appear whether or not you ask for them. For example, on many devices **findfont** will return the font `Courier` if it cannot find the font asked for. When this substitution is performed, a message is generated back to the host computer that looks like this:

StoneSans not found, using Courier.

If a PostScript error is triggered, the standard error handler produces a message back to the host system containing the name of the error and the token that triggered it:

%%[Error: typecheck; OffendingCommand: if]%%

Printer management software should be prepared for any kind of text that may be sent back from the printer. Here is a reasonable approach for dealing with these messages:

- If the text is thought to be an error message, it should be communicated back to whatever software submitted the job to be printed, or displayed for the user to see.

- If the text is not an error message, then it should be compared to a list of known standard messages that may be issued by that printer (as listed in the Printer Description File). Some of these may safely be ignored.

- If the text is not recognized, it should be communicated back to the application which submitted the job, and/or saved in a disk file and made accessible to the user.

- Under many circumstances, a disk file containing everything that the printer sent back to the host may be appropriate, both as an error log and as a way to extract specific bits of information from the printer.

There are messages which are more or less standard depending on the physical capabilities of the printing device. For example, following are a number of relatively common (self-explanatory) messages. These are all very device-specific, and the Printer Description File should be consulted for a precise list of them for a given printer, as in the following list:

%%[PrinterError: out of paper]%%
%%[PrinterError: cover open]%%
%%[PrinterError: warming up]%%
%%[PrinterError: out of toner]%%
%%[PrinterError: paper jam]%%
%%[PrinterError: recorder not responding]%%

These messages are similar in syntax to the PostScript execution error messages, but are only issued when the marking engine is not ready to print a page for some reason.

As an aside, it is generally not a good idea to issue the **executive** operator (available on most devices) while in batch mode. The **executive** operator is intended for interactive use; it echoes back everything typed, permits simple line editing, and presents a prompt. Batch jobs are not guaranteed to run precisely the same way in executive mode (due to the nature of command-line editing) and it is therefore not recommended for tracking the execution of a file. It is, however, quite handy for typing short PostScript language sequences and observing the results.

12.4 USING **EXITSERVER**

exitserver is a specialized and environment-dependent system operator available in most devices which support batch PostScript jobs (it is not part of the standard language definition). Its purpose is to exit the server loop (described in section 2.9). The **exitserver** operator requires a password, and will result in an **invalidpassword** error if the incorrect password is given.

Since the job server loop is generally responsible for cleaning up the state of the interpreter between jobs, any changes that are made *outside* the server loop by using **exitserver** will remain as part of the permanent state of the interpreter for all subsequent jobs. This only applies to changes to VM (like procedure definitions), since the stacks and graphics state are cleared after each job.

Note:

*The **exitserver** operator is a system-level command. It is not intended for general use by applications programs. Using **exitserver** is forbidden in conforming documents. See section 10.1 for further information on conformance specifications.*

The **exitserver** mechanism can be used to download fonts or procedure bodies that will stay resident in the printer until the device is powered off. **exitserver** also is required for changing any of the persistent parameters such as communications protocols or default conditions (such as the default job timeout value).

Using **exitserver** initiates a new PostScript job. It should always be the first line of code in the program. The condition of being outside the server loop persists until the next *end-of-file* indication is read by the interpreter. Any changes made to the state of VM during the job will remain until the interpreter is restarted.

Here is the necessary PostScript language sequence to exit the server loop:

```
serverdict begin
0 exitserver
```

The **exitserver** operator resides in the **serverdict** dictionary, and this dictionary must be made available in order to execute **exitserver**. It is not necessary to use **end** to remove it from the dictionary stack—when the new job is started the contents of all of the stacks are cleared.

In this example, **0** is placed on the operand stack as the password required by **exitserver**. This password generally may be changed by using the **setpassword** operator.

12.5 MANAGING FILES AND FONTS

A print spooler may be called upon to manage external resources like downloadable fonts or files. For instance, when a print file is spooled, it typically will not have embedded font descriptions (downloadable fonts) in the document file itself. Certainly in a highly distributed environment each workstation should not have local copies of the fonts.

When a document is submitted for printing, the font requirements (resource needs) are communicated along with the document, usually in the form of document structuring comments (see chapter 10 and section 6.4). This list of needed fonts (or files) is compared to the list of available fonts in the printer, and any fonts that are not already resident in the device should be downloaded along with the document file.

There are several specific structuring conventions which apply in this situation, and it is worth going through them in detail.

%%DocumentFonts

The **%%DocumentFonts** comment is used in the header section of the comments (or it may be deferred to the trailer). It should give a list of all fonts that are used by the document (if a **findfont** is performed on the font name anywhere in the document, it should be in this list). Here is an example of its use (notice the %%+ syntax for continuation; the lines should not exceed 255 characters in length):

```
%!PS-Adobe-2.0
%%DocumentFonts: Courier Times-Roman
%%+ StoneSerif
%%+ StoneSerif-SemiboldItalic
%%+ Optima
%%EndComments
```

This comment may be used first to determine if there are any font needs that are not resolved within the document. If all the fonts in this list are determined to be resident in the PostScript device, no further attention is necessary.

%%IncludeFont

This comment can appear anywhere within the body of a PostScript document file. It is a resource request. The named font should be inserted at exactly the point in the file that the comment is found (if it is determined that the font is not resident; otherwise **%%IncludeFont** can be ignored). The list of fonts for which the **%%IncludeFont** comment is used is made available in the document's header comments section through the comment **%%DocumentNeededFonts**. This has the same syntax as the **%%DocumentFonts** comment (see *listing 12-1*).

listing 12-1 ————————————————————————

```
%!PS-Adobe-2.0
%%DocumentFonts: Courier Times-Roman
%%+ StoneSerif
%%+ StoneSerif-SemiboldItalic
%%+ Optima
%%DocumentNeededFonts: Optima
%%+ StoneSerif
%%EndComments
%%EndProlog
%%Page: 1 1
 save
%%IncludeFont: Optima
 restore
%%Page: 2 2
 save
%%IncludeFont: Optima
%%IncludeFont: StoneSerif
 restore
%%Trailer
```

These comments are *directives*. If they name fonts that are determined not to be resident in the printer, then the requests need to be satisfied, or the document will not print successfully.

%%BeginFont, %%EndFont

When a downloadable font file is embedded in a document file (either before it reaches the print spooler, or by the spooler itself), the font should be bracketed with **%%BeginFont** and **%%EndFont** comments. The **%%DocumentSuppliedFonts** comment should be used to indicate the names of any fonts supplied within the body of the document:

```
%!PS-Adobe-2.0
%%DocumentFonts: Sonata
%%DocumentSuppliedFonts: Sonata
%%EndComments
%%EndProlog
 save
%%BeginFont: Sonata
  % Sonata font file is embedded here
%%EndFont
 restore
%%Trailer
```

The file should execute correctly without any attention by the print spooler, since the font is supplied within the document. However, there are a few ways in which the spooler might benefit by using these comments:

- The fonts may be collected and stored in the spooler's font area for later use with **%%IncludeFont** comments.

- The fonts may be removed from the print stream if they are determined to already be resident in the printer. However, the fonts should always be replaced by an instance of **%%IncludeFont** so that it is reversible.

Whenever a font is added or deleted from a print file, the comments should be adjusted accordingly. **%%IncludeFont** and **%%BeginFont/%%EndFont** are essentially inverses of one another (each should be replaced by the other, as appropriate).

There are exactly analogous comments and operations defined for files. Details on these can be found in the specification of the PostScript Document Structuring Conventions.

12.6 DETERMINING WHAT FONTS ARE AVAILABLE

PostScript printers have many options for storing fonts. They may be built into the interpreter's initial VM (in ROM, for instance), they may be available on a built-in file system, in font cartridges (a special case of the file system) or available on a network font server. Fonts can also be downloaded to printers on a semi-permanent basis into user VM (with **exitserver**). It is not a trivial task to determine what fonts are available on a given printer.

Host-resident software should keep track of the fonts that are resident in a printer, and at best should make its list visible to (and editable by) the user. Fonts that are built into a printer (in ROM) are always available, and are detailed in the Printer Description File for that printer (see Section 12.8).

listing 12-2 ────────────────────────────────

```
%!PS-Adobe-2.0 ExitServer
%%EndComments
/$timestamp where { %if
    pop
    (time is: ) print  $timestamp = flush
    stop  % stop the current job
} if
%%BeginExitServer: 0
 serverdict begin 0 exitserver
%%EndExitServer
/$timestamp (Tue Oct 27 17:53:43 PST 1987) def
%%Trailer
%%EOF
```

A good approach to managing the list of currently available fonts is to query the printer for the initial list of fonts, and to keep that list available. If a font is downloaded to the printer, the list should be updated. If the printer is restarted, the list should be re-generated. Noticing that the printer has restarted can be accomplished by placing a *time stamp* in the printer, then checking for it each time a new connection to the printer is opened (*listing 12-2*).

12.7   HANDLING RESOURCE SHORTAGES

It is possible that a spooler will be presented with a file to print for which it cannot find (or invoke) all the necessary resources. For instance, the requested paper size may not be available, or a needed font. There are basically three ways to handle this situation:

1. *Reject the file* (issue an error condition of some kind).

2. *Substitute another resource* (scale to fit on letter-sized paper, for instance, or default to a different font).

3. *"Trust me."* Sometimes the user knows more than the software, and it should always be possible to force the spooler to pass the file through untouched. For instance, a new font storage device might be in place, but the spooler may not know how to find those fonts and will want to substitute Courier.

The *substitution* option is the most difficult to accomplish, and may or may not be advisable, depending on the circumstances. Most people will not be happy if they ask for Univers and you give them Helvetica. The pages may wind up in the trash anyway, and it might have been better simply to reject the job in the first place (and save paper). The software at least should announce its intentions in a loud voice if it is going to substitute one resource for another.

In any case, the method used to determine whether or not the resources are available may not allow for every option and something like the "trust me" in the list above should be made possible.

12.8   PRINTER DESCRIPTION FILES

The problem of keeping track of different PostScript printers and their various features, fonts, and capabilities is not an easy task. Beyond the core of the PostScript language, there are many differences between one product and another. The most important of these differences are formalized in *Printer Description Files* (available from printer vendors and from Adobe Systems). These files contain a list of the features of the printers and the necessary PostScript code to invoke them properly. Here are the kinds of features which are supported through these files:

- *Paper Sizes.* Printers may support various different paper sizes, paper trays, and even continuous-feed rolls of paper, which can virtually be any size. These are detailed in Printer Description files by keywords indicating the paper size. There is also a great deal of information on the dimensions and imageable regions of each paper size.

- *Resident Fonts.* A list of all the fonts that come standard in the printer, including the version number and whether or not it has a standard encoding vector.

- *Query Strings*: these are miniature PostScript programs that will query the device for the presence or state of many of the features found in the file (for example, whether a particular font is available, or the current paper tray).

- *Available Memory.* This provides the amount of memory available in the initial configuration of the printer.

- *Special Resources*: this includes the availability of a resident file system, variable paper sizing, the default **exit-server** password, and others.

The details on the format of Printer Description Files are kept in a separate document entitled *PostScript Printer Description Files,* which is available from Adobe Systems.

chapter 13

MEMORY AND FILE
RESOURCE MANAGEMENT

While memory holds a seat
In this distracted globe. Remember thee!
Yea, from the table of my memory
I'll wipe away all trivial fond records.

– William Shakespeare

13.1 MEMORY STRUCTURE

Writable memory in a PostScript interpreter is referred to as *virtual memory*, or "VM." It is the memory that is used for all aspects of program execution that require information storage. VM is used for storing dictionary entries, downloadable fonts, frame buffers, the operand stack, string bodies, and anything else that requires memory.

When a PostScript interpreter starts up, it allocates a large amount of the available memory for internal processing. The details of this allocation are device-specific, but in many implementations they are roughly as follows:

area of virtual memory	size in bytes
operand stack	4,000
dictionary stack	160
execution stack	2,000
userdict	4,000
8.5 x 11 inch frame buffer	1,051,875

There is typically anywhere from about 200 kilobytes to several megabytes of usable VM after the interpreter is initialized. The **vmstatus** operator can be used to determine the amount of free memory in the interpreter.

13.2 MEMORY ALLOCATION

Memory can be allocated either *implicitly* or *explicitly*. Essentially all memory is allocated by the creation of composite objects. There are several PostScript operators that explicitly allocate VM:

string   array   dict
}   ]

The **}** and **]** operators allocate memory in the same way that **array** does. Each of them counts down to the topmost **mark** on the stack and is equivalent to the PostScript sequence **counttomark array astore**.

Memory is *implicitly* allocated primarily by the creation of *literal string* bodies. For example, the following PostScript segment allocates approximately 24 bytes of VM:

(This is a literal string) show

Since the **show** operator consumes the string object on the operand stack, the string object is lost and the string body is floating in VM somewhere. The memory allocated is *not* reclaimed except by the **save** and **restore** operators.

The amount of VM used by any particular PostScript data structure is implementation-specific. In current PostScript interpreters, VM usage is approximately as follows:

operator name	bytes per element
array	8
string	1
dict	20

For example, each of the following allocates 80 bytes of memory in a current implementation:

80 string

4 dict

```
10 array

[ 1 2 3 4 5 6 7 8 9 10 ]

true { %if
        exch pop 3 -1 roll exch
        show 0 10 rmoveto
} if
```

It is good to understand the ways in which memory is allocated in order to be able to conserve it. It is not generally true that you can first get a program to work and then go back and add some kind of memory management. Since **save** and **restore** are the mechanism for controlling memory use, and since they affect *more* than just the use of memory, this must be designed in from the start.

13.3 SAVE AND RESTORE

The only way to manage memory is with **save** and **restore**. All VM used since the previous **save** is reclaimed when **restore** is executed, including the contents of dictionaries and arrays. The **save** and **restore** mechanism should be used as often as necessary to reclaim memory.

The **save** and **restore** operators affect all other aspects of the state of the interpreter, including the *graphics state*. It is best to use **save** and **restore** in an integrated fashion to preserve both graphics state and the contents of VM between logically independent elements of a PostScript program. There is a discussion of the use of **save** and **restore** in Section 6.3 relating to modular program design.

SAVE OBJECTS

The **save** and **restore** mechanism works in a somewhat unusual fashion. The **save** operator produces what is known as a *save object*. This object is like a coat check coupon—in order to get your save level back, you must present the save object to the clerk.

A save object contains a "generation number" that is assigned sequentially. It is possible to restore to any save level by presenting the appropriate save object to the **restore** operator, but restoring level 1 makes levels 2 and 3 no longer valid (for obvious reasons).

Since **save** produces an object and **restore** requires one, they can be used somewhat like **gsave** and **grestore**. However, the save object must stay on the operand stack:

```
save
    count 1 eq { (save object is on stack) = } if
restore
```

Since the save object must be presented to **restore**, it is usually better to store it in a dictionary than to leave it on the operand stack for an extended period of time:

```
/saveobj save def
    count 1 eq { %ifelse
        (save object is on stack) =
    }{ %else
        (save object is NOT on stack) =
    } ifelse
saveobj restore
```

The sequence **/saveobj save def** seems a little unusual at first. Since **save** produces an object on the stack, and since **/saveobj** is just a name object resting on the operand stack, it is a simple definition. The **save** does not affect the operand stack, and since the name object is created before the **save**, it does not affect the state of VM that is saved. The object is then retrieved by that name when it is needed later.

THE **INVALIDRESTORE** ERROR

The **restore** operator can trigger one error condition which can be quite difficult to debug: the **invalidrestore** error. There is only one condition which will provoke this error, but there are several ways to achieve it.

The **restore** operator restores the entire state of memory back to a previously saved state. All objects in memory which have been created more recently than that save state are discarded. The condition which provokes an **invalidrestore** error is a *com-*

posite object on one of the stacks (operand stack, dictionary stack, or execution stack) that *points to* a value in memory somewhere that *would be reclaimed* by the **restore** operation. Since **restore** does not affect any of the stacks, it is considered to be an error condition for an object there to have its composite value removed from under it.

The **invalidrestore** error can be prevented simply by never leaving a composite object on any of the stacks that was created more recently than the last save level (at least, don't have it on one of the stacks if you are about to do a **restore**). The most common of these, actually, is to leave a dictionary on the dictionary stack. For example, the following PostScript fragment provokes the **invalidrestore** error:

```
save
    /mydict 28 dict def
    mydict begin
restore
```

It is difficult to get a composite object onto the execution stack that would cause an **invalidrestore**, but it is possible. Since the most likely object to find on the execution stack is a procedure body, this is the place to look (particularly innocent procedure bodies like those presented to **ifelse**). The following example provokes an **invalidrestore** error because the remainder of the procedure body in which the **restore** is found is still on the execution stack when **restore** is executed, but it was created more recently than the save object.

```
save
Ypos 36 lt { restore showpage } if
```

The only way to prevent this is to define the procedure *before* the save is executed, or not to execute **restore** from within the procedure. For example, the following short procedure definition fixes the problem:

```
/restorestate {
    Ypos 36 lt { restore showpage } if
} bind def
save
restorestate
```

13.4 DOWNLOADABLE FONT PROGRAMS

Downloadable fonts are simply PostScript programs. In general the programs build a data structure and then register it as a *font*. A downloadable font program is conceptually like this:

127 dict begin   % allocate a font dictionary
/FontName /TestFont def
/BuildChar { } def
% ...
currentdict end
/TestFont exch definefont pop

The **definefont** operator takes a font dictionary and registers it in the list of fonts available to **findfont**. This includes making an entry in a dictionary known as **FontDirectory** which contains the association between the font name and the font dictionary. Font dictionaries are allocated from VM in exactly the same way that any other dictionaries are allocated, and use memory from the same pool.

The only way to reclaim the memory used by a downloadable font is with **save** and **restore**, since the space occupied by a font is in the form of a dictionary. Each element of a font dictionary may require more memory, as well. For instance, the entry in a font which provides the font matrix requires memory to store the matrix itself:

/FontMatrix [.001 0 0 .001 0 0] def

This requires about (8*6 = 48) bytes of memory. Note that the 8 bytes or so required for the *array object* itself was already allocated to the dictionary in which it is stored. Its existence on the operand stack requires no further VM. A typical Adobe downloadable font dictionary requires approximately 30 kbytes of VM.

13.5 PACKED ARRAYS

In all but the very first implementation of the PostScript interpreter, there is a feature known as *packed arrays*. This feature is a storage optimization that permits arrays to be stored in much less space than standard arrays. A packed array is *read-only*. All array operators other than **put** and **putinterval** will work with packed arrays. In general, sequential access to packed arrays is as fast as with normal arrays, but random access is slower. Packed arrays are typically about 50 to 75 percent smaller than their unpacked counterparts.

Packed arrays are perfectly suited for procedure bodies, which are read-only arrays. A typical way to use packed arrays is to turn the feature on at the beginning of the prologue definitions, and turn it back off at the end of the prologue, so that all the procedure bodies created in the prologue will be stored as packed arrays, saving space:

```
%!PS-Adobe-2.0
%%EndComments
/setpacking where {
      /currpack currentpacking def
      pop true setpacking
} if
/prologue { packed array procedures } bind def
/setpacking where {
      pop currpack setpacking
} if
%%EndProlog
%%Trailer
```

All procedure bodies constructed while packing is set to **true** will be packed arrays. There is also an operator called **packedarray** which is analogous to the **array** operator, except that it constructs a packed array object instead of an array object. This is a more specific operator that can be used to allocate a single packed array object; the **setpacking** operator is more appropriate for general use.

13.6 RASTER MEMORY

Frame buffers (or, in some devices, band buffers) are large chunks of memory set aside as raster memory (or display memory). Frame buffers are used essentially as device space for some PostScript interpreters. Frame buffers are typically allocated by the **framedevice** operator, although there is already typically a default frame buffer in place for each device. The **framedevice** operator takes a specified width and height and allocates the entire chunk of memory necessary for rendering that page size. It is *not* a recommended operator, however.

The amount of memory required for a frame buffer can be determined easily. One byte of memory contains 8 bits of information, each of which is used as a pixel in device space (unless it is a grayscale or color device, in which case there may be many bits per pixel). An 8-1/2 inch by 11 inch frame buffer on a 300 dot-per-inch printer requires the following amount of memory:

$$\frac{300 \; (8.5 \times 11)}{8}$$

This is 1,051,875 bytes of memory (just over one megabyte). Changing page sizes therefore can affect the amount of usable memory that is available for a user job.

13.7   FILE SYSTEMS AND DISK MANAGEMENT

PostScript interpreters that have a file system available can use this secondary storage for many different purposes. Typically the font cache is permitted to occupy space on the disk as well as in the fixed partition of memory normally used for the character bitmaps. Additionally, a high-resolution PostScript devices may use the disk for raster storage when it runs out of space in memory. Finally, downloadable font programs can usually reside on the file system.

For the most part, disk management is limited to the user partition of the file system. This is the space available for downloaded fonts and other user-defined disk files. The system partition is used for the font cache and perhaps for raster storage. The PostScript language supplement for any particular device should provide details on these operations.

13.8   POSTSCRIPT LANGUAGE FILE OPERATIONS

The PostScript language has full software support for file systems. There are PostScript operators for opening, reading, writing, and closing file streams present in all implementations of PostScript interpreters.

Many PostScript devices do not have a file system available to them directly (unless there is a disk and file system built into the printer, for instance). However, the *input stream* and *output stream* are treated as file objects, and the file operators may be used to read and write these streams.

THE STANDARD INPUT STREAM

The input stream is directly accessible to user programs as a file object. The **currentfile** operator returns a file object representing the current input stream. The PostScript interpreter uses the same file object for interpreting your program, but *there is only one file pointer*. This means that the file can contain both data and executable PostScript language statements.

Listing 13-1 is a short example of how a program can read data from the current file.

listing 13-1 ─────────────────────────

```
%!PS-Adobe-2.0
%%Title: currentfile example
/buff 128 string def
/F { findfont exch scalefont setfont } def
%%EndProlog
12 /Helvetica F
10 10 moveto
currentfile buff readline
This line is actually data
pop show
showpage
%%Trailer
```

The interpreter scans and executes the **currentfile** operator, which produces a file object and leaves it on the operand stack. The interpreter then executes **buff**, which places a string object on the stack. Then **readline** is scanned and executed.

The file pointer for the input stream is left at the point just after the **readline** token. When **readline** is executed, the file object from which it reads is the one left by **currentfile** (the standard input stream). The **readline** operator picks up exactly where the interpreter left off, and reads one line of input (In this case, it reads the string **This line is actually data** into the input buffer **buff**). When **readline** finishes, it has advanced the file pointer to a position just after the line of data, and the interpreter picks up where **readline** left off. The interpreter then scans and executes **pop** and **show**, which prints the data string at location **10 10** on the current page.

This technique of reading from the current input stream is used in many ways. It can be used by a printer emulator to read data intended for a different printer. It may be used to read bitmap data for the **image** operator directly from the input stream (using **readhexstring** rather than **readline**).

Listing 13-2 contains a short program that reads a font program from the current file and writes it to a disk file, assuming that a file system is available to the PostScript interpreter. The file name needs to be changed for each different font downloaded (this is done by a front-end program). Since the program reads through end-of-file, it must be in a job by itself. Subsequent jobs can then access the font from the file system simply by calling **findfont**. This example uses the font from *listing 9-3*.

listing 13-2 —————————————————————————————

```
%!PS-Adobe-2.0
%%Title: writetodisk.ps
%%EndComments
/buff 128 string def
/fd (fonts/Logo-Font) (w) file def
{ %loop
    currentfile buff readstring { %ifelse
        fd exch writestring
    }{ %else
        dup length 0 gt { %ifelse
            fd exch writestring
        }{ %else
```

```
                    pop
               } ifelse
               fd closefile
               exit
          } ifelse
} bind
% file should follow the "loop" token....
loop
%%BeginFont: Logo-Font 1.0 0
 12 dict begin  % leave one empty slot for FID
      /FontName /Logo-Font def
      /FontMatrix [ 1 0 0 1 0 0 ] def
      /FontType 3 def
      /FontBBox [ -5 -12 85 50 ] def
      /BuildChar { %def
          exch begin
               70 0 -5 -12 85 50 setcachedevice
               Encoding exch get load exec
          end
      } bind def
      /Encoding 256 array %def
          dup 0 1 255 { /.notdef put dup } for pop
          dup 71 /logo put  % "G" character
      def
       /logo { %def
          % draw at current point
          20 0 moveto
          gsave
               /Times-Roman findfont
               48 scalefont setfont
               (G) show -13.5 -14.5 rmoveto (R) show
          grestore
          -4 -8 rmoveto
          /Helvetica findfont 11 scalefont setfont
          (glenn) show 22 3 rmoveto (reid) show
      } bind def
 currentdict end
 dup /FontName get exch definefont pop
%%EndFont: Logo-Font
```

chapter 14

ERROR HANDLING

Reason and experiment have been
indulged, and error has fled before them.

– Thomas Jefferson

14.1 INTRODUCTION

Programs written in the PostScript language are extremely portable. They are high-level source code intended to be executed on any number of different PostScript interpreter, even if the software that produces the program cannot physically be hooked up to the particular device.

This chapter addresses some tactics for making PostScript programs as robust as possible. It does not specifically address printer differences and portability issues, which are dealt with in other chapters. The focus is placed instead on the error handling capabilities of the PostScript language and how this mechanism can be used to advantage in applications programs.

14.2 STRATEGIES

The kind of errors that can be caught by an error handling strategy are typically *execution errors*. Assuming that the program produced by the application has been debugged to a reasonable degree, there are only a few possible failure modes which can arise in the PostScript language environment.

NON-STANDARD OPERATORS

One possible source of error is to make reference to a specialized operator that takes advantage of a feature that may not be present in all implementations of the PostScript interpreter (typically giving rise to the **undefined** error). For instance, invoking a printer-specific feature like manual paper feed or a particular paper tray will not work on a printer which does not offer that feature. A simple mechanism to avoid this is to use the **known** operator to check for the existence of the operator before you use it:

> **statusdict /ledgertray known { %ifelse**
> > **statusdict begin**
> > > **ledgertray**
> > **end**
> **}{ %else**
> > **90 rotate 0 -612 translate**
> > **612 792 div dup scale**
> **} ifelse**

This tests to see if the **ledgertray** operator exists in statusdict. If it does, it is invoked. If it does not, then the standard letter-size page is placed into landscape mode and scaled down to simulate the layout of **ledgertray**. The **where** operator may also be used in a similar fashion.

IMPLEMENTATION LIMITS EXCEEDED

A **limitcheck** error can arise if an internal limitation has been exceeded by a user program. This can occur, for instance, when using **clip**, **charpath**, or **flattenpath**. These operators are all sensitive to the *resolution* of the PostScript device to some extent. Both **clip** and **charpath** provide a *flattened* path, which means that all curve segments in the path are reduced to line segments. The current *flatness* affects the closeness of the approximation. There will typically be many more line segments when flattening a path on a high resolution device than on a low resolution device. For example, *figure 14.1* shows a curved path stroked first with gray at the normal flatness, then in black with a flatness of five user units (about 100 device units at 1270 dpi).

There are other circumstances and operators which can provoke the **limitcheck** error, of course. Operations which are sensitive to the resolution or amount of available memory may be susceptible to provoking a **limitcheck** error on one PostScript device but not another. With extremely complex paths, operators like **stroke** and **fill** can provoke **limitcheck** errors, although it is rare. This typically only happens when printing at especially high resolution. The next section describes the use of the **stopped** operator, which may be used to catch this kind of execution error.

Another error which can arise when implementation limits are exceeded is **VMerror**. This means simply that the PostScript interpreter has run out of memory. Unfortunately, this error is not always caught by all versions of the PostScript interpreter (depending on what was being executed when it ran out of memory). One symptom of exceeding the memory of a PostScript device may be that the interpreter will restart without explanation. **VMerrors** can be avoided by proper use of **save** and **restore**.

figure 14.1

14.3   THE **STOPPED** OPERATOR

The **stopped** operator provides a method for regaining control of the program when the **stop** operator is executed. As discussed in section 14.4, the default behavior of all error operators is to store some of the state of the machine in an error dictionary and to execute **stop**.

The **stopped** operator takes any executable object on the stack (usually a procedure body, but it could also be an executable file object). It copies that object to the execution stack (like **exec**) and executes it. The **stopped** operator determines whether or not **stop** was executed, places a boolean on the top of the stack, and returns control to the interpreter. *Listing 14-1* is an example of using **stopped** to catch a **limitcheck** operation on a **flattenpath** operation.

listing 14-1 ─────────────────────────

```
%!PS-Adobe-2.0
%%Title: stopped-example
%%EndComments
/STROKE { %def
    currentflat
    { %loop
        { flattenpath } stopped { %ifelse
            currentflat 1 add setflat
            ("limitcheck" on "flattenpath": ) print
            (trying again with flatness of ) print
            currentflat (    ) cvs = flush
        }{ %else
            exit
        } ifelse
    } bind loop
    stroke
    setflat % restore original flatness
} bind def
%%EndProlog
%%Page: 1 1
% build a complicated path:
0 1 30 { %for
    12 exch 2 mul translate
    20 0 moveto 0 0 20 0 360 arc
} for
STROKE
showpage
%%Trailer
```

This program will **loop** until the **flattenpath** operation succeeds. When it fails, the flatness is increased slightly and the procedure tries **flattenpath** again. This approach can be used to catch any kind of error, although it is complicated enough that it is only encouraged under some circumstances.

Another use of the **stopped** operator is to catch possible execution errors in included PostScript files. For instance, if your application contains a feature for including arbitrary PostScript files from other applications (or potentially hand-written code), it might be worthwhile to trap the errors and take some suitable action. A procedure called **userexec** is defined in *listing 14-2* that will execute any object in the **stopped** context and return control to the procedure when it has finished (even if it terminates with an error).

listing 14-2 ————————————————————————————

```
%!PS-Adobe-2.0
%%Title: userexec.ps
%%For: error handling
%%EndComments
/buff 512 string def
/p /print load def
/bp { buff cvs print } bind def
/jobdef { %def
    errordict begin /jobname exch def end
} bind def
/userexec { %def
    stopped { %ifelse
        $error /newerror get { %if
            $error begin
            (%%[Error: ) print
            /errorname load bp
            (; OffendingCommand: ) p
            /command load bp
            (; JobName: ) p
            errordict /jobname known { %ifelse
                errordict /jobname get
            }{
                (stdin)
            } ifelse
            bp
            (]%%\n) print flush
        end
```

```
                    { %loop
                        currentfile buff readline { %ifelse
                            (%ENDuserexec) eq { exit } if
                        }{ %else
                            /UnexpectedEOF  % report error
                            errordict /rangecheck get exec
                        } ifelse
                    } loop
                } if  % if newerror is true
            }{ %else
        % end of file must have been reached.  Is this an
        % error? Sometimes it means the improper use of
        % "currentfile readstring" and/or "image."
            } ifelse
            $error /newerror false put
} bind def
%%EndProlog
 (ORIGjob) jobdef
% execute some included job directly in-line:
/svobj save def
(USERjob) jobdef
currentfile cvx userexec
%%BeginDocument: included.ps
  %!PS
  %%Title: included.ps
  %%For: triggering an error
  /var1 10 def
  /var2 20 def
  %%EndProlog
  %%Page: 1 1
  var1 var2
  triggererror
  more program statements
  which should be ignored
  showpage
  %%Trailer
%%EndDocument
  % should never get this far:
  (USERjob completed.\n) print flush
  stop
%ENDuserexec

% here is where ORIGjob picks up again
  svobj restore  % will restore ORIGjob name, too
(Continuing with ) print
errordict /jobname get print (\n) print flush
%%Trailer
```

When an error is encountered, the **userexec** procedure must flush the rest of the included illustration. This is done by searching the rest of the file for a line containing only the string **%ENDuserexec**. This string would have been inserted at the end of the included code by the document composition software. The search is accomplished in this case with the **readline** and **eq** operators.

14.4 THE ERROR HANDLING MECHANISM

The PostScript language has a built-in procedure defined for each possible error condition. The procedure is invoked by the error handling mechanism in the PostScript interpreter. The following are the steps that occur when the interpreter triggers an execution error:

- The error occurs (say it is a **limitcheck** error).

- The PostScript interpreter finds a procedure named **limitcheck** in a dictionary known as **errordict** and executes it.

- The **limitcheck** procedure captures the contents of the operand stack, the execution stack, and the dictionary stack and places these into **array** objects in a subdictionary of **errordict** known as **$error**.

- The *name* of the error (in this case **limitcheck**) is stored in the **$error** dictionary under the name **errorname**. Similarly, the *OffendingCommand* (the object that was executing at the time of the error) is stored in **$error** under the name **command**.

- The **limitcheck** procedure then executes **stop**, and its job is done.

Whenever **stop** is executed, control returns to the innermost **stopped** context. You can nest **stopped** contexts. In fact, the job server loop always executes user jobs with the **stopped** operator so that it can regain control when an error occurs.

The job server loop contains a standard error handling mechanism that looks for and invokes another standard procedure called **handleerror** (it expects to find it in **errordict**) whenever the **stopped** operator returns **true**. The **handleerror** procedure produces the familiar error message (by looking in **$error** for the information stored there by the error operators):

%%[Error: limitcheck; OffendingCommand: flattenpath]%%

See the next section for an example of how to redefine the **handleerror** procedure.

14.5 REDEFINING ERROR PROCEDURES

Any of the individual error procedures can be redefined to be any arbitrary PostScript procedure. In addition, the higher level **handleerror** procedure can be redefined to provide more information when an error condition is encountered. One widely used error handler prints the error message and the contents of the operand stack on the current page, for example.

Listing 14-3 is a sample program that will redefine an individual error procedure (in this case, the **limitcheck** procedure):

listing 14-3 ─────────────────────────────

```
%!PS-Adobe-2.0
%%EndComments
errordict begin
    /*limitcheck /limitcheck load def
    /limitcheck { %def
        (Free VM: ) print
        vmstatus exch sub
        == flush pop
        *limitcheck
    } bind def
end %errordict
%%Trailer
```

This procedure produces a message back to the host computer indicating the amount of free memory in the printer when the **limitcheck** error occurred, and then invokes the original **limitcheck** procedure as well (it has been saved under the name ***limitcheck** in this example).

In *listing 14-4* is an example redefinition of the **handleerror** procedure that produces a stack trace back to the host system when a PostScript error is triggered:

listing 14-4 ─────────────────────────────

```
%!PS-Adobe-2.0
%%Title: errstack.ps
%%EndComments
%%EndProlog
%%BeginSetup
/orighandleerror
    errordict /handleerror get
def
errordict begin
    /handleerror { %def
            orighandleerror
            errordict begin $error begin
                (STACK:) = flush
                currentdict /ostack known {
                    ostack aload pop
                    pstack flush clear
                } if
            end end
    } bind def
end
%%EndSetup
%%Trailer
```

This procedure calls the existing error handler, and also returns a readable representation of the operand stack back to the host system.

14.6 HANDLING ERROR MESSAGES

Software used to drive a PostScript device has a certain responsibility to handle *error messages* (or other information) sent back by the PostScript interpreter. The standard (default) condition of the error handling mechanism in most printers is to produce a well-defined message back to the host computer and to ignore everything it receives until the next end-of-file indication. If the error handler is not redefined, something reasonable must be done with the error messages. See Chapter 12 for further information on printer management issues.

Depending on the system configuration, it may not be possible to pass the error message all the way back to the originator of the print file. The correct way to notify a user that his or her print job failed will be very environment-specific. In some cases, it may be appropriate to display the error on the screen of the host workstation. In others, perhaps the message can be written into a printer log file, or an electronic mail message sent. In still others instances, perhaps an error break page can be printed by the interpreter and sent back to the original source along with whatever pages of the document might have been printed correctly.

chapter 15

DEBUGGING TECHNIQUES

If a string has one end,
then it must have another.

– /usr/games/fortune

15.1 INTRODUCTION

Since the PostScript language is interpreted, it is fairly easy to
debug programs written in the language. However, the fact that
the programs typically are executed on a remote processor (for
example, in a laser printer) can make the process a little more
difficult.

In this chapter, it is assumed that the working environment consists of a host computer connected through some kind of communications interface to a printer containing a PostScript interpreter. There are other possible situations, but this is a common
environment and one in which the debugging issues are perhaps the most difficult.

15.2 ESTABLISHING TWO-WAY COMMUNICATION

The first step in reliably debugging a PostScript application is to
build a solid connection between the host computer and the
printer. There are several levels of communication that need to
be set up and tested.

PostScript language printers should be thought of as *computers*
when setting up communications channels. In particular, full bi-
directional communication should be expected. At the simplest
level, the printer will send back *error messages* when an execution error occurs. It is also possible for a user program to generate
arbitrary amounts of information at the printer and transmit it
back to the host.

Since a large part of debugging consists of trying to determine "what really happened," establishing solid communications is always a good first step. This may consist of purchasing or writing a downloading utility program, or it may mean implementing the communications layer of your application first.

SERIAL COMMUNICATIONS

There are three main aspects to setting up good serial communications:

- Get the cable configured correctly.

- Get flow control working properly.

- Be prepared to receive information at any moment from the PostScript device.

Flow control may be implemented in software (the XON/XOFF protocol for serial connections, or a network protocol such as AppleTalk®) or it may be handled by the hardware (the DTR/DSR protocol, for example). Most PostScript devices are initially configured for software handshaking, and need explicitly to be set to handled other kinds of protocols. The following is an example that will work on most PostScript devices with serial communications (please consult the particular printer manual for possible differences):

```
serverdict begin 0 exitserver
statusdict begin
      25 9600 4 setsccbatch
end
```

In this example, **25** refers to the 25-pin connector (as opposed to the 9-pin connector, for example). **9600** is the baud rate of the communications. **4** is a number from **0** to **7** that represents a combination of parity setting and the handshaking mechanism. Values from **0** to **3** use *software* handshaking (XON/XOFF), and values from **4** to **7** will turn on hardware handshaking instead (which may not be available on all devices). The **setsccbatch** operator establishes the default serial (**scc**) communications for the given port in *batch* mode (as opposed to interactive mode).

PARALLEL COMMUNICATIONS

Parallel ports are not available on all PostScript devices. Parallel communication ports in general do not support bi-directional transmissions, so if the parallel port is used, some special care must be used to receive any messages. Some devices may allow you to open the serial port explicitly to send information back to the host, but you have to know about it and it is not supported on all devices (please consult the documentation for the individual printer for more specific information). Parallel communications probably are not the best mode to use for general debugging of PostScript programs.

PACKET NETWORK COMMUNICATIONS

Network connections like AppleTalk® or DECnet™ are available on some PostScript devices. The details of packet-switched network communications are too complex to be detailed here. Probably the best approach is to use existing network software to establish communication for debugging with this kind of network connection.

15.3 UNDERSTANDING POSTSCRIPT ERRORS

When a PostScript execution error occurs, the default action taken is to issue an error message. This message consists of two elements:

- The **Error** name. This is the name of the PostScript error that occurred—for example, **stackunderflow**.

- The **OffendingCommand**. This is the PostScript object that was being executed at the time of the error.

A PostScript error message is very specific about *what* happened, but may not tell you *why*. For example, the **moveto** operator expects to find two numbers on the operand stack, which it assumes are *x* and *y* coordinates in user space. There are only two possible execution errors that can arise from the **moveto** operator (although **moveto** will happily take any two numbers that it finds on the stack and make that the current point, regardless of what the numbers might be—this is a third kind of error):

%%[Error: typecheck; OffendingCommand: moveto]%%
%%[Error: stackunderflow; OffendingCommand: moveto]%%

Either too few items are available on the operand stack (causing **stackunderflow**) or those items are not numbers (causing a **typecheck**). It's that simple.

Understanding why some PostScript error occurred usually requires a certain amount of context. For instance, it is helpful to know some of the following things:

- What items were on the operand stack at the moment the error occurred?

- At what point in the input file did the error occur?

- What dictionaries were on the dictionary stack?

- What was the current value of some variable or aspect of the interpreter's state?

Probably the most useful of these is to determine what objects are on the operand stack. The contents of the stack usually provide all the information that is necessary to establish what the context of the error was (although a **stackunderflow** error is certainly an exception to this, since there is nothing on the operand stack). See Section 15.5 for more details on getting stack traces.

ERROR: UNDEFINED

One of the more common errors in PostScript programming is the **undefined** error. This error is generated by the PostScript interpreter if a name lookup fails or if an explicit **get**, or **load** cannot find its argument in the context of the current dictionary stack. Here are some possible causes of the **undefined** error:

- The name is spelled wrong. PostScript names are *case sensitive*. This is probably the most common problem.

- A procedure name was used before it was defined. This sometimes results when procedures are inadvertently moved in the file, or when the slash is missing from a name (see Section 2.4).

- If the name given as the **OffendingCommand** appears to be only *part* of one of the names in your program file, this may mean that the communications are not solid. If part of the file is lost on its way to the printer, the interpreter may pick up in the middle of a token, and give an error. Check especially for *flow control* problems.

- If the **get** operator is being used at all in the program, perhaps its arguments are in the wrong order or just incorrect. Oddly, the **OffendingCommand** will *not* be **get**, but will be the *key* that is passed to **get**.

- If the name being looked up is in a special dictionary (for instance, **statusdict**, **serverdict**, or a local dictionary defined by the program), that dictionary may not be on the dictionary stack. Automatic name lookup works *only* in the context of the dictionary stack. Use the **begin** operator to push dictionaries onto the dictionary stack.

- **^D**: A control-D character (decimal ASCII 04), is the end-of-file indication over most serial connections. However, it is *not* an end-of-file over networks like AppleTalk. These should be removed from the file stream. Actually, they should never be put there to begin with. (See Section 12.3.) If the byte gets through to the PostScript interpreter (across AppleTalk, for instance) it will provoke an **undefined** error.

ERROR: TYPECHECK

This is probably the most common error in PostScript programming. Typically it results from the incorrect manipulation of objects on the operand stack. Sometimes this is a result of not realizing that a given PostScript operator might *return* something to you on the stack. Here are some common causes of the **typecheck** error:

- **stringwidth** returns *both* an *x* and a *y* value. For most fonts, the *y* component is 0. If this value is not needed, it should be removed from the stack with the **pop** operator. Very often an extra integer turns up on the stack from forgetting how the **stringwidth** operator works.

- Some operators require several operands. Be careful to supply all of them, and in the correct order.

- There is a difference between an **integer** and a **real** number. Make sure you supply each operator with the correct type. This is especially important with the **idiv** operator, since early versions of the PostScript interpreter graciously permitted real operands as arguments when they should not have.

- Do not supply an **integer** where a **boolean** is required. 0 and 1 are *not* equivalent to **true** and **false**, which are genuine PostScript objects of type **booleantype**.

Use the **pstack** operator to help you debug problems with stack manipulation. Sometimes the **roll** or **exch** operators can help when operators are in the wrong order, although typically it means that the operands should have been *transmitted* in a different order.

15.4   REDEFINING BUILT-IN OPERATORS

Any of the *names* of PostScript operators may be redefined. This is done simply by defining a new value for that name in a dictionary other than **systemdict**. This can be useful for debugging purposes. (See *listing 15-1*.)

The redefinitions of **moveto** and **lineto** in this example print messages back to the host each time they are called. The original definitions of **moveto** and **lineto** are still invoked (as ***moveto** and ***lineto**), so the execution of the file is not be disturbed in any way.

The redefinitions are *local* to the **debug** dictionary. As long as that dictionary is not on the dictionary stack, these definitions are not available. Placing **debug begin** at the beginning of a document (and **end** at the end, of course, if the program gets that far) will cause the file to execute with these helpful debugging procedures available.

listing 15-1 ————————————————————————————

```
%!PS-Adobe-2.0
%%Title: pathtrace.ps
%%EndComments
/debug 10 dict def
debug begin
    /str 128 string def
    /*moveto /moveto load def
    /*lineto /lineto load def

    /moveto { %def
        (moveto: ) print
        exch dup str cvs print     % X-val
        ( ) print exch dup ==      % Y-val
        flush
        *moveto                    % execute real moveto
    } bind def
    /lineto { %def
        (lineto: ) print
        exch dup str cvs print     % X-val
        ( ) print exch dup ==      % Y-val
        flush
        *lineto                    % execute real lineto
    } bind def
end
%%EndProlog
debug begin
    100 100 translate
    100 100 moveto
    200 200 lineto
    stroke
    showpage
end
%%Trailer
```

————————————————————————————

15.5 STACK TRACES

Getting a trace of the operand stack when an error occurs provides very useful debugging information. The only reliable way to accomplish this is to redefine the error handling procedure to "dump the stack" when any error occurs. There is an example in Section 14.5 (*listing 14-4*) that redefines the **handleerror** procedure to produce a stack trace. There is also a widely available PostScript file known as "**ehandler.ps**" that provides a slightly different redefinition of this procedure to actually *print* the error and stack trace on the current page when an error occurs. This is especially useful in that the page image that is already built can be seen even if **showpage** has not been reached in the program file. This can help narrow down exactly where the error might have occurred. A listing of **ehandler.ps** is included in Appendix B.

A stack trace of the operand stack is useful for two reasons. It can help find the spot in the file that the error occurred by providing some of the context in which the error was triggered. It also helps to discover why the error happened. One of the most common errors in PostScript programs is incorrect manipulation of the operand stack. Seeing a snapshot of the stack when an error occurs helps solve this kind of error quickly.

15.6 INTERACTIVE TECHNIQUES

Under some circumstances, it is possible to interact with a PostScript interpreter directly. In some devices, there is an operator called **executive** which will provide an interactive context for PostScript programming. A prompt is provided, and simple line-editing primitives are supported (such as backspace and delete-line). This can be a particularly useful environment for testing simple algorithms or exploring the nature of the PostScript interpreter.

If a direct connection can be established with the PostScript interpreter (for instance, by hooking up a simple terminal to the printer's communications port), an interactive session can be initiated by typing ^D (control-D, or end-of-file) followed by the word **executive** (and a carriage return). The word **executive** *will not echo* back onto your screen as you type it, but the characters will be received by the PostScript interpreter. If you type it correctly, you will see a brief message and a **PS>** prompt. (If you don't, you will get an error.) From that point on (through the next end-of-file), you will be in interactive mode.

PostScript language commands received by the interpreter in interactive mode will be interpreted in the same way that batch files are interpreted, including executing procedures, printing characters, using **showpage**; the whole language is at your fingertips.

15.7 COORDINATE SYSTEM TRANSFORMATIONS

A common error in PostScript language programming that is difficult to debug is the "off-the-page" error. That is, the PostScript program may execute correctly, and a page will be printed, but the page is completely blank. Sometimes the reason for this is that the coordinate system mapping has been modified in such a way that the image is actually painted off the page somewhere. This is not an error condition to the PostScript interpreter. Any part of any image may be off the page.

Remember that, conceptually, it is *user space* that rotates, not device space. To simulate this, tape a sheet of paper to the floor in front of you, and focus your eyes on the lower left corner of the page. That is the origin of the coordinate system. If you were to perform a **90 rotate**, think of user space rotation 90 degrees *counterclockwise* (positive rotation is always counterclockwise; negative rotation is clockwise). Imagine that your head is user space. That is, rotate yourself 90 degrees counterclockwise over the page. Notice that the Y axis is now along the short edge of the paper, and it is behind you (if you are still focusing on that corner). Translations take effect along the *current* axes. For instance, to finish setting landscape mode from there, it would be necessary to add a **0 -612 translate**:

> **90 rotate**
> **0 -612 translate**

If the previous discussion makes no sense to you, don't worry; it is just one way to visualize the transformations.

The relationship between **rotate** and **scale** is *not* a commutative one. That is, you cannot reverse the order of evaluation and get the same result. There is a further discussion of coordinate system transformations in Section 9.4.

15.8 DEBUGGING MESSAGES

A helpful technique for locating the place in a program file where an error occurred is to insert messages at key points in the file. *Listing 15-2* is an example of this technique. These messages may also be put into procedure bodies, as seen in *listing 15-1*, where operators are redefined to return status information.

listing 15-2 ─────────────────────────────

```
%!PS-Adobe-2.0
%%EndComments
/msg { %def
      print (\n) print flush
} bind def
%%EndProlog
%%Page: 1 1
(Got past the prologue.) msg
%%Trailer
(made it to the trailer) msg
```

appendix A

ERROR HANDLER

```
%!PS-Adobe-2.0
% ehandler.ps -- Downloaded Error Break-page handler
% Copyright (c) 1984, 1985, 1986 Adobe Systems Incorporated.
% All Rights Reserved.

0000 % exitserver password
/$brkpage where { %ifelse
    pop pop
    (Error Handler in place - not loaded again\n)
    print flush stop
}{ %else
    dup serverdict begin
    statusdict begin checkpassword { %ifelse
        (Error Handler downloaded.\n)print flush
        exitserver
    }{ %else
        pop
        (Bad Password on loading error handler!!!\n)
        print flush stop
    } ifelse
} ifelse
/$brkpage 64 dict def $brkpage begin
/prnt { %def
    dup type /stringtype ne { =string cvs } if
    dup length 6 mul
    /tx exch def /ty 10 def
    currentpoint /toy exch def /tox exch def
    1 setgray newpath
    tox toy 2 sub moveto
    0 ty rlineto tx 0 rlineto
    0 ty neg rlineto
    closepath fill
    tox toy moveto 0 setgray show
} bind def
/nl { %def
    currentpoint exch pop lmargin exch moveto
    0 -10 rmoveto
} def
```

```
/== { /cp 0 def typeprint nl } def
/typeprint {
    dup type dup currentdict exch known {exec}{
        unknowntype
    }ifelse
} readonly def
/lmargin 72 def /rmargin 72 def
/tprint { %def
    dup length cp add rmargin gt { nl /cp 0 def } if
    dup length cp add /cp exch def
    prnt
} readonly def
/cvsprint { =string cvs tprint ( ) tprint } readonly def
/unknowntype { %def
    exch pop cvlit (??) tprint cvsprint
} readonly def
/integertype { cvsprint } readonly def
/realtype { cvsprint } readonly def
/booleantype { cvsprint } readonly def
/operatortype { (//) tprint cvsprint } readonly def
/marktype { pop (-mark- ) tprint } readonly def
/dicttype { pop (-dictionary- ) tprint } readonly def
/nulltype { pop (-null- ) tprint } readonly def
/filetype { pop (-filestream- ) tprint } readonly def
/savetype { pop (-savelevel- ) tprint } readonly def
/fonttype { pop (-fontid- ) tprint } readonly def
/nametype { %def
    dup xcheck not { (/) tprint } if cvsprint
} readonly def
/stringtype { %def
    dup rcheck { %ifelse
        (\0 tprint tprint (\) )tprint
    }{ %else
        pop (-string- ) tprint
    } ifelse
} readonly def
/arraytype { %def
    dup rcheck { %ifelse
        dup xcheck { %ifelse
            ({ ) tprint { typeprint } forall ( }) tprint
        } { %else
            ([ ) tprint { typeprint } forall ( ]) tprint
        } ifelse
    }{ %else
        pop (-array- ) tprint
```

```
        } ifelse
} readonly def
/packedarraytype { %def
    dup rcheck { %ifelse
        dup xcheck { %ifelse
            ({ ) tprint { typeprint } forall ( }) tprint
        }{ %else
            ([ ) tprint { typeprint } forall ( ]) tprint
        } ifelse
    }{ %else
        pop (-packedarray- ) tprint
    } ifelse
} readonly def
/courier /Courier findfont 10 scalefont def
/OLDhandleerror errordict /handleerror get def
end %$brkpage

/handleerror { %put
    systemdict begin $error begin $brkpage begin
    newerror { %ifelse
        /newerror false store
        vmstatus pop pop 0 ne { grestoreall } if
        initgraphics courier setfont
        lmargin 720 moveto (ERROR: ) prnt
        errorname prnt
        nl (OFFENDING COMMAND: ) prnt
        /command load prnt
        $error /ostack known { %if
            nl nl (STACK:) prnt nl nl
            $error /ostack get aload length { == } repeat
        } if
        systemdict /showpage get exec
        /newerror true store
        /OLDhandleerror load end end end exec
    }{ %else
        end end end
    } ifelse
}
dup 0 systemdict put  % replace name by actual dict object
dup 4 $brkpage put     % replace name by dict object
bind readonly

errordict 3 1 roll put  % put proc in errordict as /handleerror
```

INDEX

DISKETTE ORDER FORM

If you send this coupon (or a copy of it) to Adobe Systems, they will send you a diskette containing all of the program listings in this book. Only the numbered listings within each chapter are included on the diskette.

POSTSCRIPT LANGUAGE PROGRAM DESIGN

Please send me _____ copies of the program diskette. I have enclosed $7.00 each to cover costs of materials and mailing. Thank you.

☐ *3-1/2" Macintosh format*   ☐ *5-1/4" MS-DOS format*

☐ *Please send information on the Adobe Developers' Association*

Name _____

Organization _____

Street _____

City / State / Zip _____

Phone _____

Send To:
Green Book Diskette Offer
Adobe Systems Incorporated
1585 Charleston Road
P.O. Box 7900
Mountain View, CA 94039-7900

BOOK DESIGN

This book design is borrowed from an earlier design by Robert Ishi for the *PostScript Language Reference Manual* and was adapted by Glenn Reid to the technology at hand and the unique demands of the book.

The type used is entirely from the *Stone* family, designed at Adobe Systems by Sumner Stone, Director of Typography. Chapter headings are set in *Stone Sans Semibold* 24 point, section headings are set in *Stone Sans* 12 point, and the body text is set in 10 on 12 point *Stone Serif* with *Italic* and *SemiBold*. All example PostScript language programs and listings are set in 10 point *Stone Informal*, using the regular and *Semibold* weights.